Building 21st the Century Child

An instruction manual
based on respect,
self-confidence,
and health

By Ron V. Shuali
With David S. Levine

Published by
Open Door Publications

The 21st Century Child:
An Instruction Manual based on respect, self-confidence
and health
Copyright © 2009 by Ron V. Shuali

Published by
Open Door Publications
27 Carla Way
Lawrenceville, NJ 08648
www.OpenDoorPublications.com

Cover Design by
Sandy Gans
www.SandyToesCreative.com

ISBN: 978-0-9789782-6-6

Acknowledgements

This book is dedicated to all teachers and mothers who have the greatest responsibility and hardest job; educating the 21st Century Child. Teaching children doesn't stop for a parent once the child goes to school and vice versa for a teacher when a child leaves the classroom. We are always students and teachers simultaneously.

This acknowledgement is to the teachers who give their hearts, souls, and energy to do whatever it takes to have their students succeed. This is for the mothers whose hearts twist every time they send their child to school knowing they won't see them for another 10+ hours.

Finally I dedicate this book to my mother, and the many other mothers like her who were both parents and teachers. They had the greatest responsibility and the hardest jobs. Educating their own children alongside the many others that they taught.

I hope that my readers find value from this book.

Table of Contents

Introduction

Raising a child is one of the most difficult tasks in the world. Parents and teachers alike have the most complicated jobs, responsible for the continuous coaching and guidance of the children who are in their lives. Unlike most of the devices, machinery and equipment in the world, children don't come with an instruction manual. With those inanimate devices, the more complex they are the more complex the manual, often over a thousand pages! Sometimes it takes the operator years to learn all the ins and outs of a complex piece of equipment. Think about the first time you use a new piece of software. You make many mistakes in the beginning, but eventually you learn from those mistakes and the next time you use that software it runs more efficiently.

The brain of a child is much more complicated than any software, computer, or other piece of equipment; however, they never come with an instruction manual. There are hundreds of books on all sorts of childcare subjects ranging from nutrition, fitness and education to behavior modification and child psychology, and as an educator you have taken your share of classes in each of these subjects, as well as learning about classroom teaching techniques; but to expect a teacher to read all of the books available on the subject is impossible, and to use the trial and error method on the children as a way to evaluate which books have correct or the best information and which provide bad advice is unacceptable.

Since the beginning of time, humanity has managed to raise children successfully, and teachers have managed to teach them. Twenty years ago, many children were more respectful, responsible, and self-sufficient than the children of the 21st century. Changes in society in the last twenty to thirty years have meant changes in the way that we raise our children, which has led to changes in the way our children behave, and the way in which they must be taught in the classroom.

In the past, a one person income was sufficient for most families, and a mother was usually at home to greet their children at the end of the school day. She was there from three o'clock to six o'clock to check on homework, discuss any problems the children had with friends or in school. When the school work was done the kids went outside to play on their own for a few hours; giving them the time and place to develop their social skills with family and friends.

The economics of the 21st century have made it necessary for most of today's families to consist of two working parents. During these crucial afternoon hours, no one is home to teach those essential life skills, such as how to get along with others, how to deal with a bully, or simply making sure that homework is completed on time and to the best of the child's ability.

I became involved with children as a teacher, not a parent. I run a children's fitness educational institute. My trainers and I teach children in preschool through fifth grade. Our students learn life skills and fitness through uniquely modified soccer, yoga, and karate programs. When I first began my fitness training program my goal was to combat the growing epidemic of childhood obesity by having the children that I worked with find at least one physical activity that they enjoyed and would continue throughout their childhood and teenage years. What I quickly learned was that the biggest distraction to the flow of my classes was children who constantly interrupted class. Sometimes the problems were social, the child was so extremely shy that he or she would not participate at all with the other children, or cried throughout the class. Other times the problems were behavioral; the child constantly acted out in a variety of disruptive ways.

Now I was no angel in school; my mother could vouch for that. I also realize that every child misbehaves at some time; but, what I observed so often in my first years as a teacher was not the *typical*, occasional misbehavior. Instead, I found that I couldn't teach a class of five year olds without at least one of them constantly fighting me for the class's attention... and winning!

As I continued teaching my programs I consulted books and attended seminars on the development of the brain in children and adults. I was fascinated and continuously tried the various communication techniques I read about with my preschool students. I was also running fitness, bully prevention, and Outsmart the Stranger™ assembly programs in schools and I saw that the behavior problems of the preschool children continued on into the elementary school years.

I'm sure you've seen it too; children yelling at parents or teachers, blatantly disobeying them, or children crying continuously in a new situation and their parents, instead of helping them to adjust, coddling them in a way that only exacerbates the problem. Again, I'm not discussing the occasional average misbehavior that is to be expected even from the best behaved child. I'm talking about the children that I call "master manipulators." These are highly intelligent children who have discovered how to manipulate adults to get what they want, continuing the negative behavior they've gotten away with as toddlers and preschoolers well into elementary school. They are often labeled, medicated, and

4

eventually given up on. The sad thing is that it was not the children's fault – the adults in their lives have allowed the problems to occur.

My original concern, the childhood obesity epidemic, is still making headlines, however a greater concern exists. Our children are not being taught the life skills that are so very necessary to flourish and be successful in society and life. That's why I made a drastic shift in the direction and focus of the work I was doing. Yes, we must fight childhood obesity and help children find physical activities that they enjoy; but, we must also teach our children what they need to succeed in the future; life skills such as respect, discipline, self-control, self-motivation, team work, and leadership.

This book has been a work in progress for many years as I developed proven systems and procedures to teach children, and to teach their parents and teachers how to mold and educate them so that they will grow to be powerful, self-sufficient, mentally and physically strong, healthy teenagers and eventually happy and successful adults. If you know a child in your life who has developed negative behaviors that will hinder them in the future, the first step is acknowledging that while it is not your fault, it is your responsibility as an adult in their life to help them.

I want to awaken your nurturing instincts. Remember to truly understand a child you must try to look at life through his or her eyes. I hope that reading this book will be as much of an adventure for you as writing it was for me. I want you to open your mind to seeing the world from the eyes and thoughts of the children. In the book you will find "Life Skills Toolboxes." Each of these sections asks you to see things a different way, or provides new techniques to try with the children in your care. I ask you to be open to any new ideas you discover in these "toolboxes," and try them out before discarding them.

The Shua Structure System ideas will help you to communicate more freely with the children in your care and make them better able to communicate with you. In fact, I think that by using these techniques you will learn how to get the children you work with or live with each day to follow your instructions, not just without the tears and the tantrums, but with joy and enthusiasm.

Chapter 1: Frustration

A teacher cannot effectively focus and teach when even one child is distracting the class.

"I DON'T WANNA!" screamed Danny as he ran around the classroom, knocking toys off the shelves as he flew by. The Halloween decorations made by Danny and the other children in the class suffered some losses as well. All the children in the classroom stopped what they were doing and stared at Danny as he went into what was a far too frequent routine. His third grade teacher, Julia, chased after him as she usually did whenever this happened.

Today was show and tell day and Danny wanted to go first. The temper tantrum had started when Julia told him that it was not his turn to go first and that she had to let someone else have a turn. When Danny heard that he threw a doll at Julia's head. She'd become accustomed to dodging flying objects. Julia told him to go to the principal's office. Danny refused. This wasn't the first, second, or even the third time this type of behavior had happened. Danny was considered a "problem child" by both Julia and the principal. When his parents were brought in to the office for conferences they just said that he had the same type of outbursts at home when he didn't get his way. There was nothing they could do at home, so how did the principal expect them to make him behave at school? The conferences always ended with Danny making promises to improve his behavior, but nothing ever changed.

It was a little over a month since Julia had started teaching at Werner Elementary. The school year had started off like any other year. She had enjoyed meeting all the children and learning about them. It was a new school for Julia. She was an experienced teacher and had taught at another elementary school after college. When her children were born Julia had taken several years off from teaching. She had enjoyed being home with her children, now age two and four, but she had a passion for teaching and looked forward to her return to the classroom.

It didn't take long, however, to discover that some of the children in her classroom were anything but easy. One child had anger issues. Another threw crying tantrums at the slightest confrontation. A third child didn't talk to any children in class and only spoke to her if she spent a lot of time coaxing him – time when she was ignoring the other fifteen students in the room. Julia felt helpless that October day as she watched the vice principal finally restrain Danny and take him to the office.

That day Julia briefly had second thoughts about being a teacher. She hated the frustration and unhappiness she felt while doing a job she loved, but she didn't know what to do to help these children or to teach the other children in the class, who often spent a good part of the day working on their own, while she was busy handling the temper tantrums, tears, and destructive behavior of her few "problem children."

She thought back to the first day of school and how happy she had been. She wanted that feeling back. She also remembered her own children's recent experience while starting at their new preschool.

Chapter 2: The New School

Julia's first day of school was a very big day, not only for Julia, but for her children, four year old Zachary and two and a half year old Olivia, who were starting their first day at their new preschool. Their neighbor had recommended the Choice School to them, saying how happy her children had been there, and Julia had taken Zachary and Olivia to visit the school the day before. They had seemed happy enough at the time, but of course, Julia had stayed with them that day. Today they understood they were being left there alone.

Zachary, in particular, wasn't too happy about it, even though Julia had emphasized all the fun he would have at the preschool and all of the new friends that he would make. Once they arrived at the preschool she had to practically pry the four year old from her leg to leave him in his class. The teacher smiled a warm smile and introduced Zachary to the rest of the students. Zachary quickly turned his head away and tucked his chin into his shirt, hiding his face.

"Not this again," Julia thought, as Zachary did his 'pulling away' routine. This was his reaction every time he met new people or encountered a new situation. She leaned down to comfort him, hugging and kissing him.

"It will be all right," she said, hugging him close. "Mommy will be back soon. It's only for a little while." She continued to hold him as she spoke, reluctant to let go even when he began to wiggle and squirm.

Julia felt that she had tried to help Zachary be less of afraid to try new things or meet new people, but nothing seemed to work. If anything, instead of getting better as he got older, the situation got worse, and Zachary seemed to need more coaxing and comforting with each new experience.

The teacher looked at Zachary. "Shy, are you? We'll take care of that in no time," she said with a warm, yet confident tone.

Julia let out a "humph!" and dropped her shoulders as she thought "good luck, we've tried everything."

As Julia walked out of Zach's room to drop off Olivia, she couldn't help but think about the absolute confidence in the teacher's voice as she had contemplated helping Zachary get over his shyness. Nothing Julia had tried had worked. Her heart sank as she watched from a side window as Zachary stayed in the back of the classroom, watching her through the window too.

"The first day is the hardest one," said a voice from behind her.

Julia turned and saw a tall, slightly plump woman with long, flowing brown hair with blonde highlights standing in front of her, hand outstretched.

"Hi there, I'm Angela, the Director. I was the one who spoke to you on the phone. If I heard correctly, then that must be Zachary, and you must be Olivia," she said with a bright smile for Olivia. She put her palm out and Olivia high-fived her. "And you must be Julia," she said.

"Many children are scared for awhile until they get used to their new environment. However after a week or so, the children make friends and get so involved in their work and play that you wouldn't be able to recognize them. Look over there by the teacher," Angela said as she pointed to a bubbly, happy, blonde child who was smiling and talking to her teacher. "Daisy's first day was spent mostly hiding under her desk, but look at her now."

Julia sighed and actually began to feel a little better about leaving Zachary, knowing he was in good hands.

"Let me show you to her room," Angela said, nodding towards Olivia as they all walked over to the other side of the school. Olivia looked inside her room and as soon as Julia started to walk away, Olivia ran to her and grabbed onto her hand. Olivia would not let go of Julia's hand. Just as she had with Zachary, Julia hugged Olivia to her, whispering words of comfort. After a few minutes of tears she was able to convince Olivia to join the other children in her class with the promise that she would see her very soon. Julia turned around and walked out the door to the sounds of Olivia crying, "Mommy, Mommy!" Julia's heart sank once again as she pulled herself away from Olivia's classroom.

Angela looked at Julia and said, "Remember, the first week is the hardest. It gets a lot easier and better after that. Are you ready to start this week?" Angela asked as she raised her hand in the air and held it there.

"Is she giving me a high-five, too?" Julia thought. Julia lifted her hand to give a half hearted high-five. When her hand connected with Angela's and their eyes met, Julia felt a burst of energy and hope. She tried not to smile, but in the end, she did.

"You have to smile when you get a high-five. Try it today and you'll see. Have a great day. See you later. Your precious gifts will be treated like diamonds here," Angela said.

Julia felt reassured and started thinking about the next part of her day. Her sadness turned to excitement as she remembered that her children weren't the only ones starting at a new school that day. Julia had been an elementary school teacher for only one year before she had had Zachary. She and her husband had decided she would take about a year off to spend time with Zachary after he was born, and before she had been ready to return to teaching she'd become pregnant with Olivia. It had been four years now since her first year as a classroom teacher. She couldn't wait to teach her new third grade class. She knew she'd been lucky to find this job; a teacher had suddenly developed health problems and had decided to retire, even though school had already been in session. They had needed someone who could quickly step in and work the rest of the year. When she got the phone call, she had jumped for joy at the opportunity.

As Julia pulled into the staff parking lot an hour before the school bell was scheduled to ring, she pictured the classroom she had taught in four years before: the Thanksgiving turkey pictures, traced with the outline of the children's hands that had hung in the classroom, the children singing excitedly as they learned holiday songs for the winter festival, the hugs that she had received from her students on the last day before summer break.

Julia walked into the school and introduced herself to the secretary and principal who greeted her with a smile. Mr. Michaels had been the principal of Werner Elementary for the last seven years. Julia's impression was that he was very professional. Julia was glad to be working with him. She knew her teaching skills were a little rusty and hoped that under his leadership she would learn. She was determined to handle any situation that arose.

Her hour of prep time passed quickly and soon her new students were trickling into the classroom as their school buses pulled up. When the bell rang, Julia said, "Good morning class, my name is Mrs. Kennedy." The children in unison said, "Good morning Mrs. Kennedy." "Today *is* a good day," thought Julia as she opened up her lesson plan book.

At lunchtime Julia headed to the staff lounge to introduce herself to the other teachers. It was comfortable and after several years as a stay-at-home mom she was looking forward to spending some time each day with other adults, particularly other teachers who obviously must have the same passion she did for working with children. Two of the senior teachers sat next to each other and talked about everything but their students and school. Julia was surprised. She was so excited about teaching and wanted to talk about her lesson plans and tell the other teachers about the great ideas she had for some fun, new activities.

Julia also wanted to find out who had been Danny's teacher last year. Obviously, being new, Julia expected that some of the students would test her. She'd been prepared for that, but after only a few hours in class, Danny was already displaying particularly inappropriate behavior. He talked back every time she asked the class to do something and he harassed the other students.

"He's completely wild and undisciplined," Julia thought. "Is it just to me, or did he act this way last year too?"

Danny had thrown something at one child, pushed another, and at one point had actually gotten up and wandered down the hall while she was busy with students in the reading circle. He'd moved so quietly she wouldn't have noticed he

14

was gone if it wasn't for one of the students calling out, "Mrs. Kennedy, Danny's leaving the room again." From that comment she had an idea that this type of behavior was pretty common for Danny. The day was only half over and Julia already felt exhausted from dealing with him. She didn't remember having any children like Danny in her classroom during her first year of teaching, she told the other teachers in the lounge.

"Oh, that's not a big deal. He can be tamed. I had his older brother last year. They both have issues. He just needs some medication and he'll be fine. I hope you have an easier time convincing the parents to give him medication now that his older brother is already on it," said a teacher.

"Well at least that pair talks! This year I have one child who's so afraid of everything she won't participate at all in class, or even talk with the other children at recess," another teacher said. "If I ask her a question she looks away from me. She won't even make eye contact. Every time I try to talk with her, she just tucks her head in her shoulders and acts like she can't hear me. I don't know. I think she's got a screw loose."

The other teachers laughed, but Julia immediately thought of Zachary.

"Wow, that's kind of harsh, it just sounds like he's a little shy," Julia thought to herself, wondering if over at the preschool Zachary's teacher was saying something similar about her child. Julia continued to listen and because she was sure the older teachers had more experience than she did, she didn't offer an opinion.

"Oh yeah! I have a little boy in my class," the other third grade teacher chimed in. "He whines at the drop of a dime about anything. If he can't do something or he can't solve a problem the first time, he starts to cry. I've tried to help him, ask him what it is he doesn't understand and try to explain things to him again, but it never does any good. He never gets any better. The next time he is the least bit frustrated he just cries and whines," she stated.

Julie could hear the frustration in the teacher's voice. "He's got issues, but I don't know how to help him," she continued. "Sometimes I think maybe all he needs is a good spanking. When I was growing up if I used to cry and whine like that my mother would say, 'you either stop crying or I'm going to give you something to cry about.' It seems like I spend ninety percent of my time in the classroom helping him, and the other children get the ten percent that's left. Maybe he's ADHD, and a little Ritalin will take care of him. I'm going to schedule a parent conference and suggest it to his parents."

"I'm glad I'm retiring in a few years," added the first teacher. "Kids are just different today; so many of them have these problems. It seems like the only way to deal with it is to put them all on medication, but half the time you can't convince the parents there's an issue."

Julia was upset by what she was hearing; if these older, more experienced teachers were frustrated, how was she ever going to help the children in her classroom?

Julia headed back to her class after lunch, pondering what she had heard.

"I don't get it, I really don't get it. I thought with all their experience they'd have some good suggestions on how I can help Danny, but they don't have any better ideas. Is it the parents' fault? The children's fault? The teachers' fault? Whose fault is it?" Julia wondered.

At that moment, the doorway filled with excited smiles as all of her children rushed back into the classroom after lunch and recess. She opened the blinds and three of them, including Danny, rushed over and ran their hands through the light, smiling and giggling at the shadows they made. Julia looked at them, including Danny, and saw the happiness and purity that she felt sure the older teachers had forgotten about in their jaded discussion of "issues" and medication.

As she watched the beams of light bounce off the children, she came to a realization. "I can't blame the light for being too bright. It is what it is. However I can be in control by opening or closing the blinds. I can't blame the children for being children. I can't expect them to change by themselves. They are just a product of their environment. I, as the teacher, need to change so I can have some power to help them."

She looked at her students and said, "I'm so glad you all had a great lunch. Now we're going to talk about nouns." She pushed her troubling discussion with the other teachers to the back of her mind and made a decision to figure out a way to help Danny and the other students with similar problems.

A week later, Julia was still having problems with Danny. He continued to disrupt class, and he and two other children, each with their own set of issues, seemed to take up all of her time and energy every day, leaving little left over for the rest of the classroom.

Julia continued thinking about her students as she pulled into a spot at the Choice School and walked in to pick up her own two beautiful children. As she walked into Zachary's room, she was pleasantly surprised. Zachary was playing a circle game with the entire group, including the teacher. This was a complete change from his behavior on his first day of preschool. Zachary saw her and smiled. He ran up to her, saying, "Mommy, Mommy, I had such a fun day. I've missed you. Today we learned about math, about birds, and we learned about playing soccer and helping your team. I scored a goal in team class!"

Julia was taken back. "Team class? What do you do there?"

Zachary smiled at her and said, "We pick up our friends if they fall down."

Julia was slightly confused. "Okay we'll talk about that a little later. Let's go get Olivia." She walked to the other room and picked up Olivia.

Her two year old also had a smile on her face and yelled "Mommy!"

Julia said, "I was thinking of you all day, let's get home."

Julia made chicken and rice with peas and carrots for dinner. Olivia was very excited at the table as she started to yell, "Yes Ma'am! Yes Ma'am!" to everything Julia told her to do. Julia asked where she learned to say "ma'am," and Zachary told her that in Respect Class they learned to always use "ma'am" or 'sir."

"Respect class? Team class? This school is something else," she thought. During dinner, Olivia didn't want to eat her peas and carrots. It was a running battle that Julia had

18

almost every night. Olivia would refuse to eat some portion of her dinner and Julia would alternately coax, plead and threaten a variety of punishments if she didn't eat. Julia usually ended the meal exhausted, and half the time Olivia had not eaten most of her dinner.

Tonight, however was different. Before Julia could raise her voice, Zachary raised his index finger right at Olivia's face, stared her straight in her eyes and said, "That's a *one!*" in a firm voice. Olivia looked at her brother, stopped crying instantly and slowly brought her fork to her mouth, filled with the hated peas and carrots.

Julia was floored! Her shy little boy had just displayed such confidence and actually had his sister stop crying and gotten her to begin to eat her dinner. "What is going on in that school?" she pondered. "I need to see this for myself."

Julia was determined to find out what her children were learning at the Choice School. She didn't know exactly what it was, but she knew it was working. She thought about Danny and the other children in her classroom. She hoped their system could work there, too. The next day, she decided she would find out how.

Life Skills Toolbox

Food for Thought

•   When you are feeling sad or blue, give someone a high-five. It is hard for a person not to smile when either giving or receiving a high-five.

•   Some people forget their commitments to help others over time. Don't forget who you are and what you mean to your children.

•   It is easy to blame the children, parents, or teachers for their behaviors. It is harder to look past that so you can help them.

•   Children will amaze you if you give them the opportunity.

Chapter 3: Choice

The next day Julia had only a half day of classes so she decided to surprise Zachary and Olivia and pick them up early. As she walked in, she noticed the bright sign above the school door and wondered, "Why is it called the Choice School?"

As she entered the building, Angela's smiling face met her and Julia found herself smiling back. Angela had that effect on her. "Nice to see you here early! Your children will be so happy to see you," Angela said.

Julia told her about her early release day and her decision to surprise her children. "I was curious. Why is your school called the Choice School?" asked Julia.

Angela looked over at Julia and said, "That is because our entire philosophy is based on our children and teachers having choice. If you have a few minutes, I could explain it to you." Julia jumped at the opportunity and sat down in Angela's office.

"Would you like some coffee or tea?" Angela asked. "Coffee, please. Light and sweet is fine." Julia answered. Angela made herself a cup of tea and gave Julia her coffee. The first sip made her feel relaxed and she was ready to listen.

"Our philosophy is about choice. Every child has the opportunity to display a good behavior. Every child also has the opportunity to choose to display a bad behavior. Our job as teachers is to direct them to choose to display the positive behavior and to continuously choose to display that positive behavior so that later on in life they can choose to display those positive behaviors on their own," explained Angela.

"For example, we teach the children to keep their hands to themselves. We teach them that study habits are good, and we teach them about the value of education. We want to have them choose to continue to follow the behaviors they have learned here. We can teach a child about exercise. Later in life it may be more difficult for him to exercise. He may have to do it by himself; he may not have a support program. Those obstacles make it less likely that he will exercise. He needs to learn to choose to continue to practice good choices for himself, not just because someone else has told him to," said Angela

Angela stopped and looked at Julia with a smile on her face. "Do you like to be told what to do Julia, or do you like to choose what to do? When you get into an argument with your husband, and he tells you relax, of course you relax right away, correct?"

Julia said, "Of course not, I get even more upset."

"Exactly. Now what if instead of just telling you to do something, your husband said something like, 'I understand how upset you are; I would be downright livid if this had happened to me. I think that if you take a couple of deep breaths, you might be able to handle the situation better, but if you don't want to, you can still remain upset. I'll still help you,'" Angela suggested.

"See right there, your husband is using a lot of "if" statements that give you an opportunity to make a choice about relaxing. Having that choice would probably help you relax more, right?" Angela asked.

"Hmm," Julia said. "You are right. So I choose how to react. I choose to either get upset, or my husband could choose to handle the conversation a different way. Then I get to choose whether I want to relax or not, and that in itself gives me the freedom to relax, instead of thinking it's him trying to convince me to do something."

"Yes, you got it!" said Angela.

Julia pondered further. "So I am the one with the choice. If a child chooses to show respect, then he'll take that on instead of feeling as he is either being forced to do exactly what the teacher has told him to do or do completely the opposite. If he feels forced, even if he does do what you've told him, he'll do it with a lot of resentment, rather than feeling good about it. Yes, it makes perfect sense."

"If you want to really see choice in action, we have a bully prevention specialist coming in an hour to teach a *Breaking the Bullying Circle* assembly program for our children. We bring him in once a year to teach the children how to be powerful if they are bullied."

"I would love to!" Julia said with excitement.

After lunch, Julia sat down in the back of the auditorium with the other teachers as the presenter came out. "I hope this isn't another boring assembly," Julia thought to herself. "Some of these presenters just go through their program and talk at the kids instead of talking with them."

She was pleasantly surprised that the assembly was different from some of the others she had seen in the past. This presenter was exciting and dynamic. The children were really engaged and he brought up some very good points. He talked about how a bully was someone who was once a victim and now felt powerless so they need to build up more power by bullying someone else.

24

One of the presenter's exercises demonstrated choice perfectly. He asked for a volunteer and picked a little blonde girl wearing a yellow shirt from the group. The presenter asked the little girl, "What is your name?"

"Jennifer" she replied.

"What color is your shirt, Jennifer?"

"Yellow," she said, looking down at her shirt.

"If I said I hate your green shirt, how would you feel?"

The little girl had a funny smirk on her face and the other children started laughing.

"What's so funny?" the instructor asked.

"My shirt is yellow. It's not green."

"Were you upset when I made fun of your green shirt?" he asked again.

"No".

"Why not?" he asked.

"Because my shirt's yellow," she said loudly.

"Okay," said the instructor. "I want everybody to open your listening ears. This is how the brain works. I said something and used my words. My words flew out of my mouth, into Jennifer's ears and she made them mean WHAT?"

He looked over at Jennifer, but she shrugged her shoulders. "I don't get it," she said.

"What did you think when I said I didn't like your green shirt?" he asked.

"I thought that you couldn't see right," said Jennifer.

The children in the auditorium broke out in laughter.

"Correct!" the presenter said. "So my words flew out of my mouth. They went into your ears and you made them mean, 'He can't see right'. Good job, high-five." He held his hand up and Jennifer gave him a jumping high-five. "Great, let's do it again," he said.

"Ready," he asked. Jennifer nodded.

"I hate your red shirt," he said.

Jennifer just smirked at him. "My shirt's yellow!" she said, as all of the children in the room began to laugh again.

"Correct. So the words came out of my mouth, they flew into your ears and then you made them mean WHAT?" the instructor asked again.

"That you're being silly," said Jennifer.

 "Right. Were you upset?" asked the instructor.

"No" she said.

"Were you scared? Were you angry?" he asked.

"No."

"Got it. Let's try it one last time," he said.

This time Jennifer crossed her arms and got ready.

"I hate your yellow shirt" the presenter said.

"Grrrrrr," Jennifer growled at him, getting angry.

The sound of "Oooohhh," came from the auditorium as all of the children leaned forward in their seats to see what would happen next.

"Wow," said the presenter. "You acted differently this time."

"Yes," replied Jennifer.

"Why?" he asked.

"Because my shirt really is yellow, and you made fun of it and that made me angry."

The presenter turned to the auditorium and addressed all of the children. "The words came out of my mouth, they flew into her ears, and she made it mean WHAT?"

"I made it mean that I don't like you and you made fun of my shirt and made me angry," said Jennifer."

Everyone began to laugh at the friendly back and forth exchange between Jennifer and the presenter. He turned back to her and said, "But wait a minute. Did I do anything differently?"

"You made fun of my yellow shirt," she replied.

 The instructor said, "You're right, but I didn't do anything differently with my body or with my sounds, did I? The only thing that I did differently was to change my words. Words are just sounds."

"Yes, but you changed your words and you were mean," said Jennifer.

The instructor said to her, "Can sounds come out and boink you on your head or can sounds pinch you or scratch you?

"No." she replied.

"Right. All I did was I changed my words. All I said was I hate your yellow shirt. I didn't do anything differently. My words came out of my mouth. I could have said pickles, hamburger, cereal, peanut butter!" All the children laughed again. "You could have made that mean anything you wanted. Can my words really hurt you or make you feel pain?" he asked.

She thought about it for a moment and said, "No."

The instructor said, "Okay, now this is important so everybody open your listening ears again. Jennifer and I were just talking. If something changed between us..." as he pointed to himself and the little girl, "and nothing changed over here..." he pointed to himself, "then where did something have to change?"

All the children pointed at Jennifer.

"Right! You see, the bully's words fly out of his or her mouth, and they go into your ears. *You*," he said, pointing to Jennifer, "get to choose what to make those words mean."

Jennifer shook her head, looking confused again. "I don't get it. I don't know what you mean."

"Okay. When I said your shirt was green and red and I hated it, did you get upset?" asked the instructor.

28

"No," said Jennifer.

"But when I said your shirt was yellow and I hated it, did you feel upset or angry?"

"Yes," she nodded.

"So you see, I just used words, you heard the words, listened to them, and made them mean something, and now, who is upset?"

"Me," she said, pointing to herself.

"Okay. You see, the bully wants you to get upset. If you do not get upset, then the bully will not win. To get what he wants he will have to go and bully somebody else. When you choose to get upset because you choose to make the words mean something that hurts, you get upset and the bully wins. If you choose to make those words mean something else; if you choose to make those words be silly and ignore them, then you win, and the bully doesn't. So can the bully bully you, or do you choose to be bullied?"

"I guess I chose to be bullied?" asked Jennifer, hesitantly.

"Right! Can the bully really bully you with his words, or are you the one who chooses to get upset at the words?"

"I'm the one who chooses to get upset at the words," she answered more strongly.

"Now does it make sense to all of you?" the presenter asked the group.

The boys and girls raised their hands and a chorus of "yes" went up.

As the teachers rounded up their students and headed back to class, Angela leaned over and asked Julia, "Did that help you to see exactly what choice is about? Every day that you are teaching, every experience that you have, and in every interaction that you have with a child, you, right there in that moment, have the opportunity to choose how to react. You can choose to react to the children in your classroom in the way that many people react, with emotion, by making the child's choice be all about you, about doing exactly what you want in the way that you want them to do it. Or you can make it about them, and helping them to learn to make the right choice in every situation."

"You can choose to take a stand for that child like our teachers here at the Choice School try to do every day. They know and understand that if we reinforce that negative behavior continuously it only leads the child in a negative direction. You are the one who gets to choose. Are you a person who is going to blame the children for not understanding what you're trying to teach them? Or are you going to realize that if a child does not understand you that it's your choice to show the child a different way to learn, and therefore make your entire class better?" asked Angela.

"If the children do not understand you, then consider that you are the one who wasn't able to communicate or to teach the children. It may not be true, but if you take that attitude, you will work from a position of power. If a child is looking at you with a blank stare in her eyes as if she doesn't understand something, you need to find another way to teach that child. That is the responsible attitude. That is a responsible teacher or parent with a choice," Angela continued.

Choice

Julia thought about her fellow teachers who she had spoken with in the teacher's lounge and how they chose to focus on the negative. She promised herself she would never think that way about the children in her care.

Life Skills Toolbox

Powerless or Powerful?

• There are many ways to look at a child's actions. Looking at a particular action in a different light allows us in turn, as teachers, to choose to react differently.

• In the list on the left are the child's actions. The center box lists reactions that make us as adults, feel powerless. The actions on the right are choices that give us power and an action that can help to change the child's behavior.

• Put your own feelings on hold for the chance to help out the other person, whether it is a child, another teacher, or another parent. Give yourself permission to be powerful.

Child's Actions	Reactions That Make Me Feel Powerless	Reactions That Make Me Feel Powerful
He won't listen	He is a bad kid	What can I do to get his attention?
She won't stop crying.	She is such a whiner.	She cries because she cries. I will continue my class and hope that she will see crying doesn't get her attention.
He regularly forgets homework assignments	That parent doesn't know how to raise her.	That parent is doing the best she can. Raising kids without experience is tough. Maybe I can coach the parent.
She continues to disrupt class	That child hates me! She is doing it to bother me.	The child wants more attention. How can I get her to behave positively?

Chapter 4: Julia Goes to the Principal's Office

Two weeks before winter break Julia was summoned into the office for a meeting with the principal. Mr. Michaels was a firm, yet fair principal who had big expectations of Julia. The teacher whose class Julia had taken over had not been able to successfully handle her classroom, and he hoped that Julia, although inexperienced, would find a new approach to reach all of the children in the room. He knew simply screaming at them to behave or threatening them with punishments that the teacher didn't follow through on never worked. He had some ideas on how to improve discipline in Julia's troubled classroom, but he wanted to hear her ideas first.

Mr. Michaels sat Julia down and began, "I wanted to have this conversation with you as a review of how you have been doing in your classroom. We have great expectations for you, Julia. I've already seen that you are fulfilling some of those expectations, but in other areas, particularly behavioral, you are lacking progress.

"You've been doing a great job with your lesson plans and you're fantastic with most of the children, yet you do not have control over some of them. What I need you to do is to step up and figure out a way to deal with the children that you're having issues with in the classroom. When they are in line and behaving appropriately, then we can talk about your long term future at this school," Mr. Michaels said.

Julia was confused and stunned. She was glad that Mr. Michaels thought she was doing a good job in some areas, however she didn't know how she would change those children's behavior for the better, and now, if the problems in her class didn't improve, her job was in jeopardy.

"I wonder what the teachers at Choice would do with these kids," she thought to herself, shaking her head in frustration.

The next day, as Julia was dropping her own children at the preschool, Angela, the director, happened to see her. She stopped and said, "Julia how's it going? I haven't spoken to you in awhile. Your children are great, by the way. It seems like they're having a great time here. I hope they are telling you good things about what they learn here every day."

"The kids absolutely love it here and they love coming home and telling me about all the things that they've learned. I've even overheard some of the other parents talking about the school; they all love it, too. By the way, I didn't know that there was a yoga class available for the kids here too," Julia said.

"Yes, there is. You know we have some additional specialists who come in each week to work with the children. In addition to the regular curriculum, we also have some pretty unique concepts at this school, you know. Our philosophy encompasses training the child's body and mind as one. We think of our yoga class as a way to teach the children about meditation. While the children are having fun they also learn how to quietly meditate and to use mental visualization exercises as a way to achieve success. We have other programs too like soccer, karate and even drama. They are good exercise for the kids, but they are also a great way to teach them about respect, discipline, and self-expression."

Julia was intrigued by what she heard from Angela. "Sounds interesting, I'd love to hear more about it sometime."

"I'd love to tell you. Oh, by the way, speaking of school how's your own teaching going?" Angela asked.

Julia rolled her eyes as she thought about her recent interview with Mr. Michaels, and said, "Ugh. You don't want to know."

"Try me." Angela said.

Julia's frustration came pouring out. "It's not what I was expecting. I have teachers around me who seem to have given up on their students and are just waiting for retirement. I have children who are completely undisciplined and don't care at all about following the rules. I have a child who cries and nothing I can do can make him stop when he gets the slightest bit upset or can't do something. I have others who constantly challenge me, so that all of my time is taken up with them, and I have nothing left over for the ones who are behaving in the way that they are supposed to behave.

"I need a miracle to help these children. I watch the way they behave now and I'm afraid they will grow up to be whiny and weak adults who don't understand why things don't always go their way; or worse, they'll become undisciplined, dangerous teenagers and adults. I feel helpless because I don't know what to do. I don't know if there is any hope for some of these children," said Julia.

Julia was so upset that she looked as if she was about to cry. Angela took her into her office and closed the door. She handed Julia tissues and suggested that if she wanted to feel better and more relaxed, to lift her shoulders up and breathe in, then let them drop and breathe out. Julia tried it, repeating the exercise four or five times and was surprised at how much better she felt.

"Wasn't Olivia a bit of a crier when she first came here?" Angela asked.

Julia nodded.

"How is she now?"

Julia started to think about Olivia's behavior in the past three months, and compared it to her behavior the summer before.

"Yes, Angela was right. Olivia doesn't cry as often, now. In fact, she hadn't had a crying session in over a month.

"You are right. How could I not notice?" Julia said, almost in tears.

She took a few more deep breaths to compose herself and added, "But my principal has put me up against a wall. He wants me to make huge changes in the behavior of the children in my classroom. If I don't I'm sure he won't rehire me next year. I don't know what to do," said Julia.

"I came into your school that one day and watched the presentation and learned about your choice philosophy and I was impressed. I am blown away by all the different positive changes that are happening to my children here. Maybe I need to try some of your philosophy in my classroom. Winter break is coming up and I'll have some free time. Can I spend some time here, just observing during those weeks, to see if there's anything I can learn to help me in teaching my own class?"

Angela smiled at Julia, and said, "Of course you can. In fact, I have a couple of teachers who are taking vacation over the holidays, and I need to find a substitute teacher to fill in. You'd be helping me out, as well."

"Great!" Julia smiled.

"Come in the Monday after Christmas and we'll get you started." Angela said excitedly. Julia thanked Angela, picked up Zachary and Olivia and drove home to tell her husband the fantastic news.

Now Julia was looking forward to winter break just as much as the children were.

Life Skills Toolbox

YOU READING THIS BOOK. YES YOU! Try this breathing technique now. It will make a world of difference.

Relaxation Exercises For You and Your Students

Working with children requires focus. To be successful you must leave your outside worries behind and focus on the children you work with and the activities you are teaching them at that moment. This exercise will help you to focus your mind and put aside other concerns and worries that are keeping you from being one hundred percent present in your work.

First, try the exercise at home for five minutes at a time. Once you can bring yourself quickly to a calm state in the comfort of your home, try it in your car and at work.

At first, five minutes may seem like a long time, but think about it. When was the last time you gave yourself a gift of peace of mind?

1. Place one hand on your chest and the other on your stomach.

2. As you take your first breath in, let your stomach expand as you breathe, not your chest.

3. Breathe in slowly through your nose for 6 seconds.

4. Hold your breath for 4 seconds.

5. Breathe out slowly through your mouth for 6 seconds. Notice how your stomach deflates.

6. Repeat 10 times.

7. Continue your breathing while you picture yourself somewhere relaxing.

8. As you breathe, think about the smells, sounds, sights, tastes, and feelings that you relate to that scene.

9. Continue for 20 more breaths, and every 3 breathes say to yourself, "Peaceful Body, Peaceful Mind."

10. If you do this often, whenever you tell yourself "Peaceful Body, Peaceful Mind" your body will remember its current relaxed state and automatically return to its relaxed state.

Learning to relax will certainly help you, the adult. A similar technique can also be used to help the children in your care learn to calm themselves when they feel shy and afraid or upset and want to lose control with a temper tantrum.

Meditation for Children

1. Designate one chair in your classroom or home as the "breathing chair."

2. If the child becomes upset have him or her sit in the breathing chair. Make sure there are no distractions or stimulus in reach.

3. Instruct the child to reach down and grab a cloud of air and bring it inside himself by lifting his shoulders.

4. As he drops his shoulders have the child breathe out strongly, just like a powerful wind cloud.

5. As he breathes out, have him think of a specific moment when he showed positive behavior. Have him repeat a positive affirmation while thinking about that moment, for example, "I am a good boy," or "I am a good listener." Make sure the affirmation is phrased positively and in the present tense, the NOW.

6. Have the child repeat this several times. You can do this as a family or group exercise as well as an individual one.

Chapter 5: Respect Class

It was a cold Monday in December and the first day of winter break. Julia felt different as she walked into Choice School; instead of feeling sad because she was leaving her children, she was excited to spend the day learning about the school's teaching methods.

"Good morning and welcome to your first day as a teacher here," said Angela, greeting her with a smile and a high-five.

Julia had gotten used to the high-fives by now. "It does always make me smile," she thought to herself.

"Well, let's get started," said Angela, as she began to take Julia on a tour of the classes. "Let's visit our Respect Class."

"Respect Class? Zachary mentions that a lot. This should be interesting," Julia thought. She had no idea what to expect as they walked into a room of about fifteen four year olds. The school's karate instructor, Sensei Steve, was teaching the class.

"What is the most important thing in karate?" the instructor asked.

"RESPECT!" yelled the excited children.

"Good job," he said. He nodded toward Angela and Julia as they walked in and sat in the back, but continued on with class. Julia noticed an energetic, red-headed boy jumping up and down in place.

"And how do we show respect?" asked Sensei Steve.

The boy suddenly froze in place and quietly raised his hand as high as he could.

"I like the way Jeff is raising his hand and showing respect," said Sensei Steve. All of the children turned to look at Jeff and then raised their hands quietly, just as he was.

"So Jeff, how do we show respect?" asked Sensei Steve.

"Listening to your mommy and daddy?" Jeff answered.

"Great job!" said the instructor, enthusiastically, giving Jeff a high-five. Jeff's grin grew wide with excitement. It was obvious the young student was proud to have received such a compliment.

Angela quietly said to Julia, "Jeff is always an energetic child, however when he first came here it was difficult for him to contain his energy. He wouldn't follow directions and would constantly distract his teachers to get their attention."

"Sounds like Danny, my biggest 'problem' student. He should have gone to this school and maybe he wouldn't be the way he was now," said Julia.

Angela pointed out to Julia that instead of seats, in this class each of the students had a "spot." These were multi-colored eight-inch circles of rubber that were placed on the floor to show the children where to stand.

The spots could easily be moved around the room for different activities, but no matter what activity they were doing, all of the children knew they were always supposed to return to their own spot.

Sensei Steve led the children in a "karate song," designed to help them learn the movements and techniques of karate. Julia noticed that all of the children seemed to enjoy the singing except one little girl who stood on her spot, crying noisily.

"That is Christina," said Angela, who seemed to know right where Julia had focused. "This is her first week here," said Angela. "What do you see?"

Julia said, "I see a child crying."

"Why do you think she is crying?" Angela asked.

"Maybe she is missing her mother or is scared of something? Maybe she is scared of the karate teacher, or just of the new situation," Julia answered.

"What would you do to help Christina?" Angela asked Julia.

"I would take the child aside and ask her what is wrong. Then I would give her some extra attention and try to calm her down until she wasn't scared anymore," Julia said.

"Yes, that's how many parents and teachers would handle the situation," said Angela, smiling in a way that Julia had already learned meant, "Just watch."

Julia continued to watch as the class was taught and waited for Sensei Steve to acknowledge the crying child. She was sure this was what she had come here to see; that magic moment where the teacher would say just the right thing to Christina to help her overcome her tears and join the group. Julia continued to wait, but nothing happened. The karate instructor wasn't even paying attention to Christina. He was actually ignoring her.

"It's obviously not that he doesn't notice or can't hear her. I can hear her way over here, and he's standing much closer to her," Julia thought, starting to feel uncomfortable. "Why isn't he finding out what is wrong? Why won't he help her?"

Julia had a very positive impression of Sensei Steve when she first walked into the classroom, but now she was beginning to think that she had been wrong. "This karate teacher has no business teaching children!" she thought to herself. Thoughts of her own daughter crying without anyone attempting to comfort her ran through her mind. Julia crossed her arms over her chest to keep herself from shouting over to the teacher, "HELP HER! SEE WHAT'S WRONG!"

Sensei Steve finished the song and then began to move the colored spots around so that the children would form a circle. Christina stood crying on her circle, but when he had finished his reorganization, Christina's spot was included in the circle with all of her friends.

Still, she stood crying on her spot, unlike the rest of the children who were excited to move on to the next exercise. Sensei Steve moved around the circle with a karate hand pad. He placed the pad in front of each child, who proceeded to straighten his or her hand into a chop and hit the pad with a powerful, "AHYA!!"

"Good down chop Brian!" the instructor said, as Brian's smile instantly doubled in size. When Sensei Steve reached Christina she was still crying heavily, but she lifted her arm up, hit the pad and yelled, "AHYA!!" Sensei Steve held up his hand and Christina gave him a high-five, just as all the other children had and then continued to cry. Every time the instructor got to her, she ducked, jumped, and hit the pad as if nothing was wrong. Her crying slowly stopped as she became interested in the activity. When she stopped crying, Sensei Steve quietly handed her a tissue, without making any comments. Christina blew her nose and smiled.

The next time around the circle Sensei Steve said, "Great job," as Christina chopped the karate pad. Suddenly, she began crying again. Instead of comforting her or acknowledging her tears, as Julia expected, he ignored the tears and moved on to the next child.

Julia watched the entire scene with keen eyes. Sensei Steve moved on to a new exercise, creating an obstacle course for the children to maneuver through. Because Christina had continued to cry, he had continued to ignore her, making her rubber spot the part of the course where the children frog jumped. As the children began the obstacle course, one child jumped and stopped behind Christina. She looked at him, immediately stopped crying and began to frog jump in place with a soft "ribbit," participating in the game.

At the end of class, every child, including Christina, lined up to receive a scented stamp on their hand, high-fiving Sensei Steve as they each received their reward, "Mmmmm, chocolate!" they said, sniffing their hands at Sensei Steve's suggestion, and holding them up to each other's noses.

Christina even came up to Angela and Julia, presenting her hand for them to smell. The Christina that Julia had observed during the class and the Christina who came up to Julia and Angela seemed like two different little girls.

Julia asked Angela why she had reacted differently. "I assumed she was shy, but she came right up to you and me after the class," she said.

46

Angela responded, "We have discovered that Christina does her crying act when she is around men. She's being raised by her mother and grandmother and there haven't been many men in her life, so when she is around men she begins to cry. Unfortunately, her mother and grandmother have made the problem worse by always running to her as soon as she begins to cry, picking her up and giving her a lot of additional attention. In essence, they are rewarding her for crying by giving her more attention. "But what's going to happen when she gets to elementary school? She'll have male teachers, a gym teacher, the principal, her homeroom teacher."

"She will most likely constantly cry," Julia said.

"Correct," Angela replied, "She may quickly be labeled as a child with emotional problems. Now imagine if her fear of males continues beyond her elementary school years. If she can understand and teach herself that all males are not a threat she will go through life living with power around men, not fear."

Julia was blown away. She pictured Christina throughout her future with a fear of men, and then imagined the same girl unlearning her crying behavior and growing up as a strong, independent woman.

She was absolutely amazed at the difference in the pictures she had presented herself, and understanding the problem made her realize that what Christina really needed went against every motherly instinct that she had felt while watching Christina. She really wanted to meet Sensei Steve.

"How do you do it?" Julia asked. His handshake, she noted, was as firm as his attitude with the students in his class, but there was also a kindness in his eyes that showed his commitment to them.

"Do what?" he replied with a warm smile

"Teach the entire class while that girl cried and not run up to her and try to stop her from crying?"

"Practice, a lot of practice," he replied. "It isn't easy. Of course your first instinct is to comfort the child and see what is wrong, but you have to realize that it doesn't help the child. Christina is afraid of men, so you might think that I work with her differently than I would another child who cried for a different reason, but the principle is the same, no matter what the underlying cause.

"Children are amazing actors. They learn through trial and error what gets them the attention they want. They test repeatedly and they teach themselves. Children cry. All she was doing was crying. She wasn't hurt or in pain. You, the adult, can make that crying mean anything from sadness to fear to frustration to onions in the eyes; but that is the adult's perception and not the reality of the child's situation. Christina has learned that crying gets her what she wants; for her that is perceived protection and immediate attention. Crying might be a way for another child to get a different reward.

"The bottom line is, we know that if she doesn't break this learned behavior, it will affect her tremendously in the future. I must choose in each and every class what behaviors I want to promote. Do I promote Christina's crying, or do I take a stand for the possibility of her future greatness and power when dealing with men, personally or professionally? I know that crying is not who she really is, just a learned response to a certain situation."

Julia thanked him for his explanation and he continued, "Thank you for putting aside your opinions to see what really was going on, and not just looking at things from your perspective. The first step to being a great teacher is being a great student."

He bowed to her and Julia smiled and bowed back.

As Julia and Angela continued down the hall to another classroom, Julia said, "That was an interesting class; a Respect Class. I've never seen or heard of a class like that inside a school. I've considered putting my children in Karate, but I thought it was to promote physical fitness and sportsmanship. I've never thought of it as a Respect Class."

Angela smiled with that knowing smile that Julia had noticed before. "The thing with our school is that we don't just teach the ABC's, we also teach the life skills that are needed for a child to have a healthy, successful, and powerful life. Skills and attributes such as respect, discipline, teamwork, self-control, and even the ability to meditate, are skills that that are not often taught in schools or homes, but are very necessary for life.

"Imagine if these children are respectful to everybody. Imagine if the parents were respectful to the child. If you want respect from the child, you have to give them that same respect back. Treat children in the same way that you want them to treat you. That's the Golden Rule, right?

"One thing I've seen teachers and parents do is talk about a child when they're right in front of the child, as if the child was not even there. And I've watched sometimes, when the teachers are talking and the child's eyes are looking towards them, but the head is turned in another direction, pretending that they're focused a hundred percent on the toys. They hear everything. Can you think of a time when your children amazed you? Or said something that you never expected them to say? Every generation of children is smarter, their minds work faster, and their senses are sharper. We have to appreciate that, and we should respect that if we really want to make a difference."

Julia agreed with her. "You have some unique theories. Did you come up with them on your own?" she asked.

"Not at all. I didn't think this way when I first opened this preschool," Angela replied. "Would you like to know where I learned this?"

"Of course," said Julia excitedly.

Life Skills Toolbox

Dealing With Negative Behaviors

How do you break a child away from a negative behavior? Particularly when they have learned that they receive positive rewards from this behavior? Remember, their lives will be harder if these negative patterns still exist once they get to first grade and beyond. Some teachers who are not trained on how to handle these behaviors may pass the child on to the administration for evaluation for learning disabilities or emotional issues. Many children have been evaluated, misdiagnosed, and heavily medicated only to find out later on that their challenges are not chemical, but behavioral. Once they are labeled and medicated, it may be much harder to retrain them into more positive patterns.

I call children with behavior similar to Christina either "criers" or "shyers." Criers, like Christina, will cry constantly through an activity, even one they enjoy. By shyers I don't mean a child who may be a little reluctant in a new situation, or hesitant to speak around strangers. I am referring to the child who seems to fold his neck under his shoulder, like an ostrich, and hide from everyone. He or she will refuse to participate in any activities, to answer questions, or even acknowledge the teacher and other children.

How to Handle Criers and Shyers

LET THEM BE. If you buy into their act, they will never have a reason to change it; they will remain a crier or shyer. Many parents or teachers will give these children more attention as a way to get them to stop crying or withdrawing from the group. But giving attention only reinforces the negative behavior. It also teaches the other children that this is a great way to get your attention, too.

CRIERS

- How many times have you seen a child fall on the ground and look around for an adult before they start to cry? Watch how they pick themselves up if no one is watching.

- People see crying as a sign that something is wrong with the child, but we cry while watching movies and nothing is wrong with us. When we ignore the one child who is crying and focus on the ten children who are enjoying themselves, we teach the crier that the way to get attention is to stop crying and join the activity.

- Create a game that the child can physically become a part of. For example, as Sensei Steve did with Christina, line up spots on an obstacle course and have the child's spot be part of the obstacle course. The child will stand and cry, but may get involved as the class moves around her or him, and forget the tears.

If the child is crying in a specific area of the room move the entire class over to that area slowly, trying not to be too obvious. Eventually the child will choose whether to cry or join the group and have fun. Ignoring the crying and let the child choose to get involved.

SHYERS

- Do a fun activity that grabs the child's interest. Create the environment around them, just as with the criers. Ignore the child until he or she displays a positive action, then quickly acknowledge the child and move on.

- A common mistake is to give the Shyer a lot of attention the instant he or she displays a positive action, rather than a simple acknowledgement. This will take the typical shyer right back into his or her shell. Let the shyer adjust slowly.

Chapter 6: The Shua Structure System

"How long has Choice School been open?" Julia asked.

"Nine years in September," Angela replied. "However this school wasn't always as amazing as it is now. Of course, we were always passionate teachers who taught math, English, art and social skills. But it wasn't until the day we brought the Shua Structure System into the school that the children and teachers changed."

"What is the Shua Structure System?" Julia asked as she leaned forward in her chair.

Angela smiled and replied, "How did I know you would ask that? Well, the Shua Structure System is a complete mental and physical life skills program."

"I can see why a system like this can help any school, but sometimes I wonder why parents just don't discipline their children at home?" Julia asked out loud.

Angela replied, "That is the question of the decade! Picture this for a moment. At your office, do you have pictures of your children everywhere?"

"Of course! In my car visor, on my desk, in my purse, should I go on?" Julia sarcastically retorted.

"What time do you normally drop your children off here, eight o'clock in the morning, right?" Angela asked.

Julia nodded, "Sometimes earlier."

"Then you look at your children's beautiful pictures all day and miss them a little?" Angela asked.

"A lot!" Julia stated loudly.

"Got it, then you pick them up at six p.m., right? You drive home and start dinner. By the time dinner is done, it is seven thirty or eightish. Your children are up for another hour or so and then off to bed.

"Now picture them running around the house, playing with toys when you've asked them to head to the bath, or begging for a few minutes more to watch a television program instead of going to bed on time. Nothing major, just being typical kids, pushing your buttons, maybe being a little disrespectful," said Angela.

Julia laughed. "It happens at least three nights out of five," she said.

"Now, do you always consistently discipline them or some nights do you let them get away with it because you just feel too tired, or too stressed about work, or a little guilty because you haven't spent enough time with them that day?" asked Angela.

Julia thought for a few moments about herself and her friends who were also working mothers and realized Angela was right. All she wanted to do when she got home each night was to love them and make them happy. She didn't stop to think when she gave in to whining behavior or tears that the consequences of each of those little actions could eventually lead to undisciplined children.

Julia thought back to her own childhood and said, "When we were in school, we would come home to mom and she would ask us about our homework and once it was done she would kick us out of the house to play outside. No DVD, Internet, or computer games."

Angela said, "I cut out the internet at home when my twelve year old son told me he was going to play with his friend Tyler and then never left our house. I checked upstairs to see when he was going out to play with his friend. He pointed to the computer screen and said, 'Mom, I am playing with him. Look, I am the Orc King and he is the Dragon Warrior. We're on a quest.' I disconnected the Internet in his room the next day. He was furious with me at first, but eventually he got bored and started playing outside with his other friends. Now they play wizards and warriors with their minds and bodies outside, not inside on a computer. I even bought him and his friend's costumes for their games. What do you think about that?" Angela smiled smugly and put her hand up again for another high-five.

"Why do you always give high-fives?" Julia asked Angela. "I know that the kids enjoy it, but it seems that their karate instructor gave them out an awful lot, too."

"Interesting," Angela said. "Do you think there's something wrong with it?"

"No," Julia answered, "just a question."

"What we do in and out of our classes is to give as much positive reinforcement as possible to the students whenever they display positive actions. If a child displays a positive action continuously, we continuously give them high fives. The other reinforcers that we use are the scented stamps. They're very popular. The children love them so much that they will literally stop the negative behavior in its tracks when they're told that they're coming close to not getting a 'smelly stamp.' But you don't have to use stamps or high-fives. Another version of the same thing is a smile, a hug, or a comment like 'great job!' We all have positive reinforcers in life all the time, even adults," explained Angela.

"Really?" Julia asked.

"Of course. Every time you go to work you get a positive reinforcer every two weeks," Angela said.

Julia thought for a moment, then smiled and replied, "A paycheck?"

"Of course," Angela said. "If you didn't receive that positive reinforcer every two weeks, would you show up to work?"

"No, I wouldn't," Julia said

"Would you do a good job if you didn't get your check consistently? If one week you got your paycheck, but the next week you didn't, even though you'd worked just as hard?" Angela asked. "What if you never knew which weeks you would get that paycheck and which you wouldn't?"

"Maybe," she said, but then shook her head, "well probably not."

"What if you knew you would get a bonus if you worked harder? Would you be excited about doing your job and would you work harder than you had to?" Angela asked.

"For a guaranteed bonus, absolutely!" Julia said.

"Why do some people work harder than they have to?" Angela asked.

"Well, maybe they're hoping to get a raise," Julia replied.

"Exactly," Angela said. "They're hoping to get an additional positive reinforcer. Consistent positive reinforcement for young children leads to positive reinforcement for older children and then for adults."

Julia smiled as she thought of all the high-fives the instructor gave to the children. Angela put her hand out and Julia gave a high-five. Julia tried not to smile, but found she couldn't help it. "You have to smile. High-fives are magical!"

"Julia, remember when you were three or four years old?"

"Not really" Julia said.

"Well, can you imagine it? Picture yourself as a three year old child. What are the things you do? What are the things that three and four year olds do?" asked Angela.

"Well, they play with their friends, they eat, and they drink; they poop a lot."

"Yeah," Angela smiled and looked at her. "There's one more thing that children that age like to do. They like to test adults. They're going through a learning process and they need to see what reactions provide what outcomes. They want to learn what reactions come from their new actions, and through that they learn which behaviors get them the outcomes that they desire.

"If you were a three year old child do you think you might be a little bored sometimes? Imagine having all the energy that that three year old has and nothing to do. Sometimes televison bores them, other times playing with other kids bores them, but getting a parent upset – that's always fun.

Angela continued, "Well, let me ask you another question. Do you have somebody in your life who knows exactly how to push your buttons? Do you know that one person that you can be having a great day and then all the sudden, they just say one thing to you and your day is ruined? If you watch them closely, ruining your day has even made that person feel a little bit better."

Julia smiled and nodded, as she thought about her sister who knew exactly how to get underneath her skin no matter what the situation was. She even felt a little of that frustration just thinking about it.

"Now," Angela said, "Do you know anybody in your life whose buttons you know exactly how to push?"

Julia blushed as she thought about her husband's tender spots, and nodded to Angela.

"Children push your buttons all the time. It is kind of like you are an elevator. Some children will do with people exactly what they do with elevators, push the call button. The button lights up and then they wait. If the elevator arrives, they learn that pushing the button gets them the elevator. Some children, just like some adults, will keep pushing the button, even when they see that the light is on," smiled Angela.

"Now think about this, if the elevator would arrive faster if you pushed its button several times, wouldn't you keep pushing that button?" asked Angela.

"Of course," Julia said.

"Well if the adults come up with the proper response - the response the child is looking for - more quickly if those buttons are pushed more often, don't you think that child is going to learn to keep pushing? It doesn't take long to realize that the more he pushes, the faster he gets what he wants," Angela said.

Julia nodded. She could easily picture Zachary and Olivia or her students at school pushing her buttons faster and faster until they got the reaction they wanted from her.

"Now what if the button was pushed and the elevator never came?" continued Angela. "Eventually if that elevator doesn't arrive, do we stand there next to it waiting, or do we leave and find another way?"

"We leave it." Julia said, with a laugh.

"Exactly! So here is another choice. When a child pushes your buttons, are you going to be the elevator that gets frustrated, shows a reaction, and lets the child win? Or are you going to be that elevator that doesn't show up and makes the child choose to stop pushing your buttons?"

"Obviously I don't want my buttons pushed," Julia said strongly.

"Then choose not to let it happen," Angela said.

"What if they don't stop pushing?" Julia asked.

"That is why we use the Shua Structure System." Angela said proudly.

"The Shua Structure System?" repeated Julia, understanding.

You are a human being. You acted this way when you were young. So do all children. Choose to accept

60

children the way that they are rather than thinking, "They shouldn't be this way…"

Life Skills Toolbox

Getting Your Buttons Pushed

Children consistently do four things:

- Test you to see how you react to different behaviors

- Remember the actions that you react to

- Repeat those actions when they want your attention

- Create and find new behaviors to test on adults

First steps in changing behaviors

- Identify the behavior that you want stopped

- Ignore the behavior that you want stopped

- Inform the child of the consequence if the behavior is repeated and dare or challenge him to display the negative behavior again.

- **Follow through** with that consequence immediately if the behavior is repeated

- Publicly and loudly identify the behaviors you approve of

- Reinforce the positive actions when they are repeated

- Continue to acknowledge and focus on the child's positive behaviors

Chapter 7: Discipline

Angela started the second day of Julia's training by showing her why Zachary had said "one" when Olivia had refused to eat her peas and carrots.

"For our programs to be successful, all children must behave in a proper manner. The key is to have the children choose to show respect instead of telling them they must show it, and trying to force them into it. We implement the Shua Structure System for our students," said Angela.

"First, we explain to the children the rules and that they are put in place for their safety. An example we use is that when two boys in another class didn't listen, they accidently ran into each other and were injured. And we ask if any children want to get a 'boo-boo.' One of our rules is, 'Be a good listener,' and the children hear it repeatedly. The example shows them that they should choose to be good listeners because they do not want to bump into their friends. They make a choice themselves because they understand why they should be a good listener, instead of just being told to be a good listener.

"Second, we acknowledge required positive behavior with genuine smiles, high-fives, verbal acknowledgement and scented stamps."

"When negative behavior is displayed, we implement the Power Look. You know the look, as a Mom, I'm sure you've used it yourself," she told Julia. "Now you are going to use it intentionally. The Power Look is a non-emotional blank face that shows the child that the behavior he or she is displaying is not getting a reaction from the instructor. When you are giving the Power Look, do not look into the child's eyes. Instead, look at the top of his or her forehead so you don't get sucked in to the 'aren't I adorable' faces that so many children develop to manipulate adults with."

Angela went on to explain the rest of the rules in the Shua Structure System.

 Life Skills Toolbox

The Shua Structure System
1.   If the child is not being a good listener, he receives a verbal "one" as the instructor shows the child their index finger and the Power Look.

2.   If the child continues to display negative behavior, he gets a "two" and the Power Look.

3.   If the child continues to misbehave, he gets a "three" and is instructed to sit in the Breathing Chair. In the Breathing Chair he breathes in and out deeply while raising his shoulders up and down. He is asked to think about a previous time when he did act as a good listener. This technique teaches the child to meditate on something positive and helps him to learn to create and self-implant positive thoughts into his subconscious mind. Those positive thoughts will in turn become positive actions. The child is instructed to raise his hand when he is ready to be a good listener.

---

4.   After the child sits in the Breathing Chair for a few minutes the instructor asks the child to explain why he is there. If the child says, "I don't know," the teacher says, "When you are ready to explain you may come back to the class." Once the child has explained why and promises to be a good listener, he is allowed back with the class.

5.   Being put in the Breathing Chair bruises the child's ego in front of his peers, and that means that there may still be resentment in his thoughts even after he returns to the class. The instructor must quickly find a way to acknowledge a positive action so that the child can leave the negative feelings behind and replace them with positive emotions and feelings of success. For example, tell the child he is standing well, sitting great, playing nicely; give him a big smile with a high-five. The child has now completed an entire cycle, beginning with no response for a negative behavior, to a happy, excited response for a positive behavior.

6.   Once the child has been sent to the Breathing Chair, the number system does NOT start again. This is not baseball; it is not a new inning. If the child continues to not pay attention, he gets a "four," and is sent out of the classroom. For example, if he is in an enrichment class such as art, he can be sent back to If he is in homeroom he may need to be sent to the office. This method helps the child come to understand that to be able to participate in the class

requires positive behavior. The rules are in place and the instructor will not budge on the rules, because allowing those rules to slide is selling out on all of the children in the room.

This method has been used repeatedly to teach children with behavioral challenges to understand that there are rules in life and they need to be followed. Make the children want to be involved in class so that they will choose to be respectful, rather than trying to force or trick them into it unwillingly.

Julia assisted in an arts and crafts classroom for five-year-olds that day, and there she saw the Shua Structure System in action. A little boy by the name of Jayden began class in a rambunctious manner. His teacher gave him a "one." After he had received a *one*, Jayden fell into line, but a few minutes later he again didn't follow instructions and sit down when asked. "Two," his teacher said.

Five minutes later Julia noticed that Jayden was again out of his seat and didn't return to it when his teacher asked him to. "Three, Jayden," she said. She never took her attention from the rest of the class, continuing not only to teach the lesson but to acknowledge the other students with a high-five and a quick word of praise for positive behavior. It only took her a split second to look right at Jayden with her Power Look as she called the number, *three*.

As soon as he heard *three* Jayden headed to the room's designated Breathing Chair and sat quietly. After two minutes the teacher told the children to continue with their art project and walked over to the boy.

"Jayden, why are you in the breathing chair?" she asked.

"Because I wasn't being a good listener," he quickly replied.

"You are right," said his teacher. Now, you know in this classroom, if you want to stay here, you have to be a good listener."

Jayden put on a sad face and said, "I know."

"Okay Jayden, you know that sad face does not work here, actions work here. If I let you back into class, will you be a good listener?" she replied.

"Yes," he said, nodding his head vigorously.

He returned to his seat at the table, picked up his crayons and began to color, but it didn't last. Five minutes passed and Jayden got into an argument with one of the other children and pushed him down.

"Jayden, that's a four. You can't stay in art class today you must go back to your classroom," said his teacher.

Jayden immediately burst into tears. "I don't want to go back to my classroom," he cried.

"Jayden, you chose to break the rules," his teacher reminded him.

"But I don't want to ..."

"You chose to break the rules. Go back to your classroom," the teacher said again.

Jayden began to cry harder as all of the children stopped their work and turned to watch the scene, but he did slowly head out of the door, dragging his feet as he walked, his teacher silently following to see that he did head back to his homeroom.

As the assistant took over the classroom, getting the children back on task, Julia followed Jayden and his teacher into the hallway. She was surprised to hear the teacher say, "Jayden, make sure you go to the water fountain and get a big drink of water, that way you can cry more if you want, because you know your crying act doesn't work on me."

Jayden turned around and looked at the teacher, his tears shut off instantly, as he stared at her for a moment, then turned and headed back to his classroom. He stopped at the door, placed his hand on the door to turn the handle, and like an award winning Oscar nominee, turned the tears back on as he opened the door and walked into his classroom. From inside the classroom, they heard his teacher say, "Jayden! What happened?" as the door closed.

Jayden was able to turn the tears on and off whenever he chose, Julia realized. She was floored.

"He can turn it on and off in an instant," she thought. It was an incredible lesson for her to understand how powerful children can be when they use their emotions.

Julia thought about how she would react in a similar situation and hoped she would be able to follow through, as Jayden's teacher had. She knew she could do it on those *one's* and *two's* and even the breathing chair, but what about when she had to give a *four* and send the child out of the classroom? She knew her student Danny, would certainly test her resolve.

"You will be tested, Julia. Just remember that children love to test. That's what they are wonderful at. The thing that's going to separate you from other teachers is to first, never doubt yourself, and second, follow through on all of your promised consequences," Angela observed. "When you teach your classes, do you follow through on every single thing you say?"

Julia smiled, and said, "Of course!" in a sarcastic manner, which Angela realized meant the exact opposite.

"I know it's difficult and I understand that sometimes the process of disciplining a child is challenging," continued Angela. "For example, picture yourself telling a child that if she doesn't change her negative behavior, you'll call her mother. As you are about to pick up the phone to call, something else happens. You get distracted and go handle that situation, and then the first child is left realizing that you were going to call her mother, but you didn't. Even if the entire classroom is in chaos, in that child's world the teacher not calling her mom made a huge difference. A teacher must follow through on everything."

By Thursday of winter break, Julia was rocking and rolling. She had been practicing the Shua Structure System at home with her children and it worked like a charm. She was looking forward to the opportunity to try it in a classroom and that day she got her wish. A teacher at the Choice School called out sick and Julia was given her own class of four year olds, a lesson plan, and an assistant teacher. Things ran very smoothly. She handed out a couple of *one's* and *two's* as she taught the English and math lessons. That settled the children down. They seemed to understand that even though "Miss Julia" was just a substitute, she would follow the same discipline rules they were used to. An hour later she took the children to their Teamwork, Respect and Leadership classes and watched the instructors closely.

Later on in the day the class went to the Fun Room for exercise, movement and play. Julia led the children in a game of Tunnel, and that's when a little boy named Eddie changed her life completely.

Eddie was a bright, excitable little boy. He was very energetic and was always looking for attention from his teachers. He hugged Julia often throughout the day.

Eddie seemed unable to stay still in the fun room as Julia began the fitness program of exercises. Eddie, however, left his spot and headed over to play with a fire engine, instead.

Julia used the Power Look, aiming her eyes right at Eddie's forehead. She extended her index finger and said, "Eddie, that's *one*."

Eddie looked over at her, understood, and returned to his spot in the exercise group. Julia felt happy. Once again, the Shua Structure System was working.

But a few minutes later, Eddie again left his spot and headed over to the toy corner to play with the fire engine. "T*wo*," said Julia, giving Eddie another quick stare as she continued to lead the children in their exercises.

Eddie again returned to the group, but when it was time to start clean up, he began throwing balls at one of his friends.

"Eddie, we do not throw balls at our friends," said Julia. Eddie picked up the ball and threw it again. "Three," she said. "It's time for the breathing chair."

Eddie quietly sat in the chair as Julia reminded him to breathe and think about how he could be a good listener. When two minutes had passed, Julia let the assistant teacher lead the next part of the lesson as she went over to talk to the little boy.

"Eddie, why are you in the Breathing Chair?" she asked.

Eddie was sitting quietly, gulping deep breaths in and out. He looked at Julia, shrugged his shoulders and said, "I don't know."

"Eddie, I think you do. I want you to think some more about it," she replied. "Are you allowed to play with the fire engine when it's time for exercise?"

"No," he said.

"Eddie, are you allowed to throw balls at your friends when we are in class?"

He shook his head, no.

"Eddie, those are things that we can do when it's time for free play and I think you know that. So when you are ready to be a good listener, you can come back in to class. Please raise your hand and let me know."

Julia walked back over to the rest of the children. A minute later, Eddie raised his hand.

Julia said, "Eddie, come back in."

Eddie returned to his spot with a sad expression on his face. It tugged at Julia's heart, but instead of offering a comforting hug, she acknowledged him for standing nicely on his spot. Eddie smiled, and his mood immediately shifted from sad to happy.

When Julia asked the children to clean up, Eddie was the first to begin straightening the room and Julia quickly gave him a high-five and thanked him for being a good listener.

The next activity was jump rope, and to Julia's surprise, instead of continuing his good behavior, Eddie pushed one of his friends.

"Eddie, that's a *four*. Time to go back to your class," said Julia.

"NO!" yelled Eddie. He sat down on the floor, folded his arms and refused to move. Julia knew she couldn't stop the rest of the class to beg Eddie to do as he was told, so she quickly went across the hall to the director's office.

"Nancy," she said to Angela's assistant. "It's Eddie, I gave him a four."

"I'll be right there," said Nancy. Heading into the room she picked up the boy saying, "Eddie, I know you can be a good listener," as she walked him out of the classroom.

The next day, the regular teacher was still out sick, so Julia again taught the same group of four year olds. Their schedule for the day was similar. After arts and crafts they returned to the fun room. Before Julia started the class, she went to Eddie and said "Eddie, I know you can be a good listener if you want to be. Will you be a good listener today?"

Eddie looked at her with innocence in his brown eyes. "I'll be a good listener today," he said, putting his hand up for a high-five.

"Great! I'm very proud of you," Julia said, returning his high-five with a smile.

"Wow, that Shua Structure System works so well, now he's excited to be a good listener," Julia thought happily.

Then the strangest thing happened.

Before Julia could start the lesson and get the children onto their spots, Eddie went over to the fire engine, looked right at Julia, and began to play with it. Julia looked at Eddie in amazement. She couldn't believe what she was seeing; she was really upset, she had believed Eddie when he said he had learned his lesson the day before.

Julia took in a deep breath, calmed herself, and making sure she had her emotionless Power Look in place said, "Eddie, that's a *one*." Eddie just stared at her for a moment, and then continued to play with the fire truck.

"Eddie, please go to your spot. We do not play with the fire engine until free play. *Now that's a 'two,'*" said Julia.

Eddie did not want to listen and immediately, she said, "Eddie, that's a *three*. Go to the breathing chair."

Julia was surprised, because Eddie headed right over to the breathing chair. He sat their quietly, lifting his shoulders up and dropping them down, as he breathed in and out. Julia thought smugly to herself, "This does work. He challenged me a little, but he's really picking up that I mean business. I know with this method I'm going to whip my third graders into shape in a week. It's so easy. I wish I'd known about the Shua Structure System before."

Julia waited for two minutes, then gave the class a "Do Now" activity. This was an engaging, self-sufficient activity that would occupy the class for a few minutes when the teacher needed to tend to one individual in the room. Julia squatted down to Eddie's level and said, "Eddie why are you ...,"

But he cut her off before she could finish saying, "I wasn't being a good listener."

"You're right," said Julia, thinking a little smugly to herself, "This is really working and it's so easy."

"Eddie, if you want to be a good..." she began.

"I'll be a good listener," Eddie interrupted, again, putting his hand up for a high-five.

"Okay Eddie, I want you to show me how you could be a good listener," she said, responding to his high five.

Eddie headed back toward the other children, then passed them by without stopping and headed for the fire engine. Picking it up, he turned once to make sure that Julia was looking at him.

Julia began to get angry. "He is intentionally mocking me!" she thought and said, "Eddie, that's a *four*! I'm going to get Ms. Nancy."

Julia asked her assistant to watch the class and headed across the hall to the director's office, where Angela and Nancy were working.

"Nancy, its Eddie again, I had to give him a four," Julia said loudly enough that Eddie would hear her from inside the room. Nancy smiled and said "Okay, I'll be right there."

As Julia peeked into the classroom, she saw that Eddie was no longer playing with the fire engine. He'd moved over near the door.

"Looks like he is about to run," Julia thought. She was right. When Eddie saw Nancy enter the room, he got a big smile on his face and took off down the hall. Nancy's high-heeled shoes made a "clippity-clop" sound as she chased after Eddie. Suddenly he stopped, and Nancy scooped him up in her arms. "Eddie, you have to be a good listener," she said, as she headed back to her office with him.

As Julia watched from the door of the classroom, Eddie turned to look at her, a big grin on his face.

"What just happened? Why is Eddie smiling?" Julia thought out loud.

One of the girls in the class raised her hand. "I know, Miss Julia. Eddie loves Ms. Nancy. He likes to sit in the office with her."

Suddenly it all made sense! Something clicked and Julia realized she was finally seeing the big picture and could really understand what had happened in the last two days. She began to laugh, shaking her head, she found herself feeling a little bit in awe of Eddie and his ability to manipulate the situation.

Julia realized that it had only taken one class period for Eddie to train Julia on how to help him get what he wanted. He didn't want to participate with the class in the fun room. Instead, he preferred to sit in the office with Ms. Nancy, where he had her undivided attention.

No, Julia realized, she hadn't been training Eddie. He'd been training her!

What she had learned that day was going to make a difference in the rest of Julia's teaching career. She had never realized before how fast children could learn how to get adults to do what they want them to do. It gave her a new appreciation for her students. The week at Choice School had really helped Julia to become equipped with tools and knowledge she needed to change the behavior in her own third grade classroom.

Life Skills Toolbox

More on the Shua Structure System

This proven discipline policy can be used by both teachers and parents to help insure that the children in their care systematically choose positive behavior over negative behavior - every time. Be brave and try it with your children today. An easy way to introduce the concept is to say, "Kids, you go to school and read books to learn. So did I. I learned about rules. And this is the new rule policy. It begins now!" You can do it. YOU ARE IN CHARGE!

Additional Tips for the Shua Structure System

- Use a simple, easy to understand example to explain the reason for each rule.

- Explain the Shua Structure System to the children before you begin to use it.

- Give out *one's, two's,* and *three's,* and the Power Look to disrespectful children.

- If a child receives a *three,* tell him to sit in the Breathing Chair, breathe in and out, and think about himself as a good listener. If the child refuses to go into the breathing chair, send him back to his homeroom, or if this is not possible, find another, appropriate negative consequence that the child will not like. For example, sending a child to sit with a person that he likes, or sending him to do a task he enjoys, is not a negative consequence. If the child complains, explain that he was the one who chose to break the rules. Repeat if necessary.

- Once the child shows he wants to come back to class, talk to him until he understands that his actions are not acceptable and he promises not to be disrespectful again and to be a good listener.

- Engage the child about anything to give him the opportunity to be acknowledged for good behavior so that he feels that he is back in the good graces of the instructor.

- If the child receives a *four,* remove him from the class for the rest of the session. Do this without emotion. Then explain to the child that he will be given another chance during the next period to be good listener, and give him a high-five. This will let the child know that you still like him, even though you are laying down the law and insisting on appropriate behavior. During the next period, whether it is the next class, the next day, or the next week, the child will start with *zero* again.

Understanding a Child's Actions

If you are confused about a behavior a child is displaying, take these steps.

1. Break down the behavior into specific actions. Look for the reality of what happened and try not to put your own spin, or your own emotions into it. For example, a child throws a toy. The parent or teacher's emotional response is, "He threw that toy to upset me." The reality however can be much simpler. The child simply threw the toy. He wasn't thinking about the adult's feelings or emotions at all. Maybe he was just looking for a REACTION.

2. From the child's perspective think about what benefit or reaction that behavior will cause. Your mind can create dozens of potential reasons that the child is displaying a certain behavior. However each reason can be either very valid or just as wrong. For example, "When he throws that toy, I get angry at him. He sees my reaction and he smiles and laughs. That gets me angrier;

therefore, he must have thrown it to make me angry." However there is another possible reason. "He smiles and laughs when I get angry because he is embarrassed at his own behavior."

3.   Once you think you know the true reason for the behavior, change your reaction. Instead of acting in the way that you have in the past try a new reaction. Instead of anger, act unconcerned about the incident. **This does not mean that you do not give a consequence, such as sitting in the Breathing Chair.** It does mean that you show no emotion while explaining the consequence. If changing your reaction stops the behavior, you will begin to understand the child's motivation.

4.   To truly discover the cause of the behavior, use the "projection" technique described in the next chapter of this book. Using projection will help you to get the child to tell you why he does certain things because he is talking about them through the voice of another child.

Chapter 8: Projection

It was Julia's last day of winter break at Choice School; the next Monday she would return to her own school. She sat down to lunch with Angela, Nancy, and Diana; a school psychologist who loved her job working with the teachers and students at Choice. As they discussed the week and the various children Julia had worked with, Julia kept thinking about how what she had learned about the Shua Structure System could help her work with the children in her own third grade classroom.

"Most of the time the Shua Structure System works if the child wants to be in the classroom. If they choose to be in the classroom, they learn they must choose to follow your rules," Diana said. "However, if a child does not want to be in the classroom, and of course that does happen, particularly in the older grades where the work becomes harder and there is less playtime, the Shua Structure System still gives you ways to figure out why the child is displaying negative behavior, and how to change it.

"Let me tell you about a little boy I met about three years ago. His name was Joseph and he was four years old," said Diana. "Joseph was having problems in school; he was a little troublemaker, and by that I don't mean fighting with the other kids. Joseph was just not a good listener, Diana said, using a phrase Julia had heard a lot throughout the week and had also learned to use herself. It easily covered a whole wealth of behaviors that the children at the preschool, just like children everywhere, used as a means of doing what they wanted to do, rather than what the teacher had asked of them.

"Joseph would constantly leave his classroom and wander the hallways against the teacher's instructions," Diana continued. "His teachers tried to make him stay in his room. The director tried to make him stay in his room. The other children would yell to him, 'Joey, come back into your room!' For some reason Joseph couldn't stay still. He was quite the energetic little boy!

"Now sometimes he would be very well behaved and involved in his lessons for an hour or so, then suddenly, for no reason, he would throw an object, push someone, or have some other type of outburst. I was asked to speak to Joseph and see if I could help him. I quickly realized that a technique called, "Projection" would be the quickest way to break through and find out just what was behind his behavior," explained Diana.

"Projection is a technique that takes the focus off the particular person and places it on someone else, whether real or imaginary, so that you can get to the heart of the problem. Think about yourself sitting in a psychologist's office. The psychologist is sitting across from you ready to listen, and you know that you have one hour to tell him everything that's bothering you. Do you think there might be a slight amount of pressure on you? You don't know this person, or trust them yet. Do you think your subconscious mind will completely open up and explain everything so you can resolve the problem? Absolutely not; the mind has many locked doors to which you don't have the key, and when pressure is added, it makes it even harder to open up. It's just the same for children as it is for you or me.

"Children aren't usually comfortable lying to someone. They won't make eye contact if they are uncomfortable. They'll look off in another direction. Remember that; when a child is looking you right in your eyes, the majority of the time, unless you've got a really amazing actor on your hands, he or she is telling the truth.

"Back to Joseph; The first thing I did when I went in to talk to him about his behavior was to squat down and talk to him on his level. This is so important with young children. As the adult you are so much larger that it is easy to intimidate them. I didn't want to do that, I wanted to be on his level. The first thing I did was call him 'Joey,' and he replied, 'My name is Joseph.'

"'Then I'll always make sure I call you Joseph,' I said. If you want to receive respect from a child you must give them respect, and calling them by the name they prefer is one easy way to do that. Respecting everybody, including the children that you work with makes a huge impact on the conversations that you have with them.

"'Joseph, do you like school?' I asked. Joseph replied, 'Yes,' but he never looked up from the handheld video game he was playing. You see, he would talk to me, but he wouldn't make eye contact. 'Do you like going to your classroom?' I asked, and this time, he said 'No!' and he did look up from his game for a moment. But when I asked him why, he just shrugged his shoulders, said, 'I don't know,' and returned his attention to his game.

"I decided this would be a good time to use Projection, by creating another fictional child to discuss with Joseph. "When you use projection, make sure the child you create is similar to the boy or girl you are talking to, so that they can easily identify with your fictional child. When I was talking with Joseph I created Max.

"'Joseph,' I said, 'I have another little boy in my other class named Max, and I need your help with him. Would you like to help?' Joseph became interested. He sat up and he said, 'Yes.'

"'Max looks a little like you. He has blonde hair, and he wears the same kind of sneakers you do,' I told him. I watched Joseph, and I could see him visualizing Max," Diana explained.

"Max is a smart boy, and Max sometimes does not want to stay in his room. It is very important to Max's mommy, daddy and his teachers that Max stay in his classroom and plays with his friends. If he does not stay in his classroom, then his mommy and daddy will take him out of that school with all his friends and put him in another school where he doesn't have any friends."

Diana continued, "Now you might think this sounds like a threat, but Joseph needed to realize that there were consequences to his actions. It's possible he hadn't realized that if he didn't change his behavior he might be moved to another school. I told Joseph that I did not want that to happen to Max, because I knew Max really like his school and his friends. Then I asked Joseph if he wanted that to happen to Max. Joseph shook his head and he said 'No.'

"I started to ask Joseph questions about Max. Do you think Max doesn't like his friends?' I asked.

"'Joseph shook his head. 'No, he likes them,' he said."'Does he like his teachers?' I asked.

"'Yes,' he nodded. "'Then what could be the reason that he is always leaving the classroom and wandering around the halls? Do you think he's afraid of his classroom?' I asked.

"Joseph looked me in the eye, nodded, and said, 'Yes.'"

"'What do you think Max is afraid of?' I asked."

"'Maybe Max is afraid of the big spider by the red door," Joseph said.

"'Jackpot!' I said to myself, as Joseph led me to what I was looking for. 'Why would he be afraid of a spider?'" I asked.

"Joseph said, 'Maybe when Max was sleeping, he woke up and a spider was crawling on his neck and bit him and he got really scared.'"

"'So you're telling me that Max is afraid of a spider and that's why he doesn't like to be in his classroom?' I asked.

"Joseph nodded, 'Yes.'

"I finished talking with Joseph and told him I would be right back. I got up and walked around the corner to Joseph's room, and guess what! There was the red door of his room and there was a spider web with a big, ugly spider in it. It was a door that stayed opened all day and a spider web had formed on the bottom. The teacher hadn't noticed it. The cleaning crew hadn't noticed it. But Joseph had. I got a broom and wiped up the spider web and took the spider outside. Then I went back to Joseph and said, 'Joseph, can you show me what kind of red door you think Max is afraid of?' Joseph said 'Okay,' and took my hand and walked slowly to his room.

"I said, 'Could you show me where the spider would be?'"

86

"Joseph hesitated, then told me where to look. He wouldn't look himself. I told him I didn't see a spider. Joseph walked around and looked. To his amazement, there was no spider there. Joseph smiled, walked into the room and began to play with his friends. The teachers were amazed. I explained that all along the problem had been the spider.

"You see," said Diana, "Projection is a technique that you can use when you need to find out the real reason behind a child's behavior. It is much easier for children to explain their own behavior through the lips of another child. Don't forget, sometimes it works very well with puppets, too, rather than creating another child."

 Life Skills Toolbox

Using Projection

1. **BUILD RAPPORT:** Make eye contact with the child. Get down to his or her level and create rapport with the child. Start the conversation by talking about a safe subject, anything that does not have to do with the subject that is troubling the child, until he or she begins to feel comfortable with you.

2. **CREATE ANOTHER CHILD:** Start talking about another child, like Max, and mention that this child has similar physical characteristics and clothing.

3.   **ENGAGE YOUR CHILD INTO CHOOSING TO HELP THE OTHER CHILD:** Ask your child if he is interested in helping that other child. Most likely he or she will agree as a way to take the focus off of themselves. If they agree, continue, if they do not, you may have to try at another time. This process cannot be forced.

4.   EXPLAIN THE CONSEQUENCES OF THE OTHER CHILD'S ACTIONS TO YOUR CHILD: Joseph hadn't realized that his actions might make his parents move him to another school.

5.   **LEAD YOUR CHILD INTO A CONVERSATION ABOUT WHY THE OTHER CHILD TAKES THESE ACTIONS:** Ask him why he thinks that child is taking those actions. Coach him. The child will usually explain the feeling behind what is going on with the fictional child you have created. After that, try to get the child to explain the cause and see if you can change the situation so that the child will no longer need to use the negative behavior.

6.   **COACH THE CHILD ONCE THE PROBLEM IS DISCOVERED:** Use your teaching abilities and show the child how to solve the problem.

Projection

Chapter 9: Good Boy/Bad Boy

"One of the most important things his teachers noticed about Joseph's behavior," continued Diana, "was that sometimes he displayed perfect good boy characteristics; he was focused, energetic, helpful, respectful and polite. Then something would happen. He would just switch instantly from good behavior to bad behavior. Before talking with him I watched him interact with his friends and I saw a shift occur when he was bored or wasn't focused on something. He would throw a chair, run and slide down the hallway, or suddenly act out with his friends. We had discovered a trigger for the situation – the spider. But I still needed to follow up and find out more about Joseph and why he would switch his behavior so suddenly.

"Joseph wanted to help out with Max, so later that day I spoke with him again. I said, 'Joseph, let me ask you a question. Sometimes Max throws chairs or slides on the floor when he should be sitting still. Why do you think he does that? Joseph, do you think Max is a good boy?'" I asked.

"Joseph continued to play with his toy while refusing to make eye contact. He said, 'Yes.'"

"I knew he didn't really believe what he said or he would have looked me in the eyes. 'Can you please look me in the eyes?' I asked. 'Do you think Max is a bad boy?'

"Joseph looked right at me and his face became emotionless," said Diana.

"'Max is a bad boy,' he said very firmly. He got up and said, 'I don't want to talk about Max anymore!' and left the room.

"I went to the director and explained to her what I had learned. In Joseph's world, Joseph was a bad boy. Earlier in the day I had seen him walking around the hallways and one of the girls pointed to Joseph and said, 'Joey's a bad boy!' Sometimes his teachers also would say, 'Joey's a bad boy,' and even his mom would tell him, 'Joey's a bad boy,' when he misbehaved. When children constantly hear that they are bad boys or girls, they believe it. What kind of actions does a bad boy take? Bad boy actions," said Diana.

"I knew that Joseph thought he was a bad boy, and if he didn't change that perception, he would continue being a bad boy for a long, long time. I didn't know where that might lead him, what school he'd be put in, what psychologist he'd have to constantly see, or what medication people would try to put him on. I needed to take a stand for Joseph right there, and I chose to help him.

"Joseph suddenly reappeared in my office and told me he wanted to talk about Max again. I was so happy and excited. 'Thank you,' I said, and we spent several minutes talking about Max and the toys Joseph thought Max liked to play with. After five minutes I asked another question.

"'Joseph, are you a good boy?' I said in a happy and cheery way.

"Joseph again intentionally avoided making eye contact with me and said, 'Yes.'

"I knew that to help Joseph I had to press forward. 'Now Joseph, if you really want to help me with Max; I need you to answer this question. Can you please look me in my eyes?' I said.

"Joseph hesitated and I let him be. He tried to keep his eyes on me, but they kept darting around as he struggled to focus. Once he did I acknowledged his focus by saying, 'Joseph, I like the way you are looking at me with your eyes. Great job!' And I smiled at him and continued on," explained Diana.

"'Can you tell me something? Are you a bad boy?' And Joseph, with the same dead pan look as before, looked up at me and said, 'I'm a bad boy.'

"I saw his seriousness loud and clear. Unless you were in his world, behind his eyes, you could never know the amount of negative reinforcement that must have happened to make him believe he was a bad boy. A few months? One year? Two years? No one knows. In Joseph's world, he was a bad boy.

"When I paid attention, I could see that when Joseph was focused and engaged, when he was having a great time, he forgot that he was supposed to be a bad boy. Then, the instant that either the focus was not on him or that he had time to relax, suddenly he shifted mentally, as if reminding himself that he was a bad boy. Then he would take his 'bad boy' actions.

"I told Joseph, 'I'm going to tell you something very, very important. Can you listen and look at me very quietly?' He looked up and I could tell when our eyes made contact that Joseph was paying attention. I said 'Joseph, there is no such thing as a bad boy. There are only bad ways to be. I'm going to say it again: There is no such thing as a bad boy; only bad ways to be. Sometimes we don't know that we're being a bad listener, and that's why teachers help us. So every time that you think you're a bad boy, you can do something to stop it. You do not have to stop it, but you can. Joseph, I'm

92

afraid that if you stay thinking that you are a bad boy, then mommy and daddy will have to take you out of this school and put you in another school like Max.'

"Some people may think this is too much for a four year old to comprehend, but Joseph understood. He understood clearly. He understood that he needed to make a choice to help himself.

"The final component to handling the good boy/bad boy situation was to teach Joseph to meditate the negative behavior away and replace it with effective positive affirmations.

"Have you seen our meditation class? It is also referred to as the yoga class?" Diana asked Julia.

Julia replied, "Only one class. It was incredible to see those extremely energetic children lie down to do their belly breathing with bean bags on their stomachs."

"Perfect!" Diana said. "That is what I was hoping you saw. In the yoga program here at the school our children are taught to visualize and meditate. The children are taught to breathe in and breathe out and say positive affirmations that will then transfer from their conscious mind to their subconscious mind.

"When I was talking with Joseph I said, 'Joseph, if you want to be a good boy, anytime you think you're a bad boy or any time you're about to do something bad, try to remember that you do not have to. This is what I want you to do. I want you to sit in a chair and lift your shoulders up to your ears and take a deep breath in' – and I demonstrated – 'and as you breathe out, say to yourself, I'm a good boy.'

"I had him try it, and he did twice, very quietly. By the third breathe I could see his excitement increase, and by the fifth time he was smiling. I looked at him and he looked at me and I think he understood. In that moment Joseph got it. I asked him if he had to be a bad boy or if he had a choice about being a good boy or a bad boy. Joseph took one more deep breath in and as he breathed out and his shoulders dropped, he said, 'I'm a good boy!' with a smile and happiness that hadn't been there before.

"I followed up with the school's director over the next few months to see how Joseph was doing. She told me that sometimes Joseph would go back to his old ways, but often she caught him doing his breathing. His mother was also reinforcing what was taught at the school and after a few weeks Joseph's behavior started to shift.

"That day I realized that sometimes it takes a special kind of teacher to step out of her comfort zone and make the commitment to take a stand for a child. Sometimes taking a stand for that child's potential greatness beyond what the teacher is comfortable with is needed, and when the teacher goes out of their comfort zone to try to make a difference for a child, that child's potential is exponential."

Julia was speechless. "Thank you so much. You have no idea how much I am looking forward to trying this when I get back to my classroom. I am certainly going to miss being around this school next week, however I am excited to try all these new tools out. Thank you so much."

Life Skills Toolbox

Good Boy/Bad Boy Strategy

When children display negative behaviors sporadically or without warning, they may believe that they are bad children. This belief may stem from constantly hearing others (family members, teachers, other children) calling them a bad boy or girl. If a child truly believes he or she is a bad child, he or she will display bad child actions. The child's parents and teachers need to be alert to the situation and explain to the child that he or she can choose to act in a different way.

1. Ask your child if he thinks the invented child you have created is a good boy or girl. If the child says, "He is a good boy" and cannot look you directly in the eyes, he may be lying. If he cannot keep eye contact ask him to look directly at your eyes and repeat the question.

2. If the child thinks the invented child is a bad boy, ask the child if he himself thinks he is a good boy or a bad boy. Make sure the child maintains eye contact for the truth.

3. If the child believes he is a bad boy, explain that there are no bad boys, just bad behaviors.

4.   After the child understands he can choose to be a good boy, have him meditate.

5.   Tell him to breathe in deeply while lifting the shoulders up to his ears.

6.   Breathe out and let the shoulders drop.

7.   Instruct the child to say out loud while he is

breathing, "I am a good boy" and simultaneously think about a time when he was a good boy. Help him choose a time when he was a good boy.

8.   Have the child repeat the breathing and the mental visualization.

9.   Continue to remind the child about the breathing when you see them begin to show a bad boy behavior.

Chapter 10: Actors

One Saturday in early January, Julia's son Zachary was invited to an indoor soccer and sports birthday party. What she saw that day would amaze her and confirm her new understanding that children often train their parents and teachers in the same way that Eddie, her student during her week at the Choice School, had trained her.

The party began with fifteen children and fifteen soccer balls on the field. The instructor hired for the party allowed the children to run across the entire area, practicing their dribbling. While most of the children were playing in a group, others were on their own, dribbling at their own pace.

It seemed as if everyone was having fun, Julia thought as she sat down to have a soft drink with another parent. Then she noticed one little boy running across the field, his arms outstretched as if he was about to tackle someone. Julia saw one of the girls kicking a soccer ball around, just having a good time by herself. She knew what was going to happen; she felt as if she was watching a sports replay in slow motion as she yelled, "No!" But before she could do anything the little boy had connected and knocked over the girl, who fell to the ground and began to cry.

The scene followed a predictable pattern. The little boy's mother ran up to him, furious. She grabbed him by his shoulder and spun him around, yelling, as she asked him why he had pushed the girl over.

He gave her a wide-eyed look, "I'm sorry," he told his mom using his best puppy dog look on his mother.

"Now, you tell her that you're sorry," said the mom, pointing to the little girl who was still on the ground crying. He turned and looked at her; however, Julia noticed that as soon as his back was to his mother, his face changed. He no longer had that cute little, "I'm sorry," expression he had shown his mother. Once again, he could see the same expression on his face she had seen just before he knocked down the girl, and Julia knew he really had meant to knock the girl down; it hadn't been an accident.

"I'm sorry," he mumbled to the girl.

His mother, not seeing his face but hearing his words, said, "Fine, I don't want to see you do that again." She walked away and the little boy got up, started to play and almost immediately knocked over another child.

Julia was astounded by how well the boy had been able to manipulate and train his mother into believing that he was really sorry. Julia thought, "If I put myself in that child's shoes, the words 'I'm sorry' are just two words that he has learned. He has realized that he can do anything that's wrong or inappropriate as long as he says 'I'm sorry.' He can pretty much do whatever he likes, and mom will believe that he's really sorry, and there won't be any consequences. He's developed into such an amazing actor that Robert Dinero would look at that child and say, 'You, you're good.'

"The down side for the child who learns that "I'm sorry" is the out for everything is that when he or she gets older, it won't always work. "I'm sorry" is not going to work when others, less gullible than his mother, realize that his "I'm sorry" is not genuine.

Julia was so amazed with her insights that when she picked up her children from pre-school on Monday, she told Angela the story.

Angela smiled and said, "Now you see the brilliance of the children of this generation. Now you understand what kind of caring teacher it takes to teach these children the rights and wrongs and the rules and life skills that are necessary. You are learning so quickly. It's a shame I have to give you back to your own school," she added with a wink.

Julia thought about Danny, her own "problem child" in her third grade class. She was already seeing new steps and solutions she could take to help him. While she was thinking about him, she felt herself becoming nervous and frustrated at the same time. She regularly talked with Angela about her students when she picked up Zachary and Olivia. One day Julia had asked Angela, "Why is it that sometimes even though I know I'm supposed to be disciplining the children, I get so frustrated that they're not listening that I don't know what to do? Do you have any insight on that?"

Angela grinned at Julia and said, "You already know the answer to that. When the bullying specialist came in, you told me that the lesson to be learned was that you are the one who chooses how to react. If that is true, then you are the one who chooses to get frustrated. Just ask yourself, is it the child who is making you frustrated, or is it that you are choosing to react to a certain situation and get frustrated?"

Julia said with a sigh, "It's me. I know that. But why do I get frustrated? That child will suffer because of their negative actions, not me."

Angela looked at her, smiled again and spoke, "Consider that the frustration that you have is not because the child is being undisciplined. Consider that the frustration that you have is not from the child, but from yourself. You know from experience that if that child does not change their behavior it will affect them tremendously in life. Consider that your perception of your inability to educate the child is what's getting you frustrated and upset and not the actual child's behavior."

"What we tell the teachers is they should thank that child. I look at it as the child just raised their hand and said, 'excuse me Mr. or Mrs. teacher, I have a discipline issue and I need help.' See, that's how we choose to look at it. Not like some of the teachers that would look at that child as just a troublemaker."

"Wow", Julia said and smiled, "That's amazing. I never thought of that. I never thought that it would go so deep, but it makes sense. I want these children to succeed so badly. I want them to get rid of their negative behaviors so quickly so that they don't have to deal with these situations in first, second or third grades and I feel that sometimes I'm not connecting with them."

Angela looked at her and smiled. "You are connecting." She said, "Every child picks up differently. Some children are auditory learners, some are visual, and some are kinesthetic learners. The auditory learner learns by hearing. The visual learner learns by seeing. The kinesthetic learner learns by movements and actions. If you really want to try to connect with the child, try to connect in all three modes. Try to teach the child with sound. If that doesn't work teach them with visualizations and pictures. If that doesn't work then physically manipulate the child's body or move them in the way that you want them to behave. Then acknowledge them with a positive reinforcer like a "good job" or a high-five.

"Make sure when you tell them "Good job!" you're telling them the specific reason why they are doing a good job. Not just in general."

"Whoa. Slow Down!" Julia said, "Let me see if I have this correct first. We teach them that their negative behaviors will not be responded to with a negative emotional reaction. Then we have the children choose to be good listeners through our coaching and their choice. And they understand that a positive behavior leads to a positive consequence, and a negative behavior leads to a negative consequence." Angela nodded vigorously.

"Got it!" Julia exclaimed. "But once we can get the children to stop displaying negative behavior, how do we get them to show the behaviors we want?"

"Great question. Most teachers never get to that question because they are still stuck in the past with the negative behaviors. We get them to display the actions we want by telling them, or pre-framing."

Life Skills Toolbox

Calling Them on Their Act

Learn to understand the "act" that many children, particularly the ones that I call Master Manipulators, use to get a certain reaction from an adult or another child. The reaction can be a form of "pushing the buttons" of the other person, or it can be an attempt to get out of a punishment or receive something from the other person.

The child's "act" is the actions that he displays when trying to get another child or an adult to react in a certain way. Once the child's act is understood, the adult can deal with the situation by telling that child that the act doesn't work and that he or she should use words instead. For example, a child who constantly jumps up and down and disrupts things to get the teacher's attention needs to be shown how to raise his hand quietly and say, "Excuse me," instead.

- Call the child on his or her act.

- If you see a repeated behavior pattern, separate the perceived reason for the behavior from the actual behavior.

For example, four-year-old Jennifer starts to cry

when she is told to listen. Instead of attempting to get her to stop crying, in other words, falling for her act, tell her that crying does not work and that she needs to use her words to get what she wants. Have her breathe in and out as you talk to her.

The same goes when a child is being disrespectful. Tell them that their old action will not work with you, but that words do. Stick to your word and try to talk to the child if they physically stop their action. Acknowledge the child and repeat the reinforcement.

Actors

Chapter 11 - Pre-framing

"Pre-framing is the easiest and most magical answer to get children to display the behaviors we want," explained Angela. "We tell them exactly what we want them to do. You see, when you give an instruction with a 'don't' the children usually will tune out the 'don't' and instead listen to everything that comes after it.

"We do this as adults, too. I'll give you an example. Don't think about an ice cream sundae. Don't think about how cold and refreshing it would be. Don't think about how creamy the whipped topping is. Don't think about your favorite sauce dripping down the sides. Don't think about the sprinkles and the cherries on top. Now, is your mouth watering?"

Julia nodded vigorously.

"Mine sure is. It's just the same with children. We want to give the children specific instructions on what *to do*, not on what we don't want them to do.

"The way to do this is called pre-framing. It is a way to give the children the information that they need so that they are successful in any action that they take. Let me give you an example; the most effective pre-frame that we use here at Choice School is the phrase, 'I like the way.'

"When you say 'I like the way' and add an instruction, watch how the children react to that instruction. For example, picture four children standing on spots in a line in front of the teacher. One child in the group falls on the ground and puts the spot on her head. Obviously that child wants attention. The average teacher will say to the child 'Will you please stand up?' then, 'Get up!' and finally, 'If you don't stand up...'

"However, often the teacher never realizes that she is focusing all of the attention on that one child who is displaying the negative behavior. The other children who are displaying the correct behavior are not getting attention, while the child who is acting in an incorrect manner is getting all of it. If that continues, the other children will learn how to get attention by mimicking the first child.

"Instead, we teach our teachers to do the following:

"Point to one of the children who are standing correctly and say, 'I like the way YOU are standing on your spot.' Point to the next child and say 'I like the way YOU are standing on your spot.' Point to the third child and say, 'I like the way YOU are standing on your spot.' That fourth child will pop up and stand in her spot immediately if they haven't done so already. Why? Because children just want to be liked. It is a basic human need. When you first started your new job wasn't there some deep down desire, even if it was a small one, to be liked by your new boss and co-workers? You want other people to like you wherever you go. When you go to McDonald's, you want the person who is giving you your food to like you. Why? Because you want to be liked by everyone. Children have that quality at a much higher level than adults. If you just tell them that you like something that they are doing, even if they're not doing it, they will start doing it because they want you to like them," continued Angela.

Life Skills Toolbox

Here's an easy way to use this technique.

Make a statement, such as "I like people who raise their hands." Now ask it as a question, "I like people who WHAT?"

Make sure you repeat the question using the exact same phrasing that you used when you made the statement.

Now that you've asked it as a question, your students will answer, "Raise their hands!"

Here's another example. The teacher says, "Everybody sit down on their bottoms. Everybody sit down on their WHAT?"

The children say "bottom." Every time the children repeat an answer that the teacher has pre-framed and they receive an acknowledgement with a positive reinforcer they instantly feel successful. Every single time this happens they feel praised and accepted.

When you are pre-framing, elevate your voice when you are stating the action you want.

Elevating the voice will give the children the hint about what you are looking for. For example, if you say, "Do I want you to sit down or I do want you to STAND UP?" Elevating the "stand up" portion of the sentence will give the children the clue that you want them to repeat the phrase "stand up!"

Even though, in this example, the teacher gave the children a choice of response, the children will guess the correct answer because the teacher's voice is elevated and her vocal expression is more excited.

Here's another example, "Do I want you to do some science now or do I want you to do MATH?" When the teacher asks this question she should add a big smile, hand movements and excitement when she says the word "math." This gives the students the visual, kinesthetic, and auditory clues that they need. The children will say "MATH!" with the same excitement that the teacher showed.

Now, think about a child receiving a high-fives or some other type of positive reinforcement such as a smile, or the words, "That's great," twenty, thirty, or forty times in a forty-five minute class, each time he or she is successful. How do you think the children are going to feel in that class? They are going to feel great because the teacher is taking the time to pre-frame them, as long as the teacher focuses on the positive and does not react to the negative the children will continue on the right path.

109

Another essential ingredient in pre-framing is to exaggerate your head movements, nodding and shaking, when asking questions to give the child another major hint about the behavior that is wanted. Shaking or nodding the head yes or no at the appropriate times helps the child knows

Enjoying the Learning Process

The purpose of educating and teaching a child is for that child to continuously learn and process new information and have it available when needed. Whether they are learning something physical or mental, the more they enjoy the learning process, the stronger the information and the more willingly it is retained. When a child isn't enjoying the learning process, he or she must work harder to learn the information and is more likely to quit trying. We pre-frame children so that they continuously feel happy and successful and want to learn more and more. Simply stated, pre-framing is telling the child the answer or desired behavior and having them repeat it back, giving them a tremendous feeling of success and continuous reinforcement.

Chapter 12: I'LL Try!

Julia was back in her own classroom. She was excited and a little scared about trying out her new tools in her classroom. She began the day with a huge smile and engaged all the children with talk about their winter break. She was determined to be friendly with her students, including the ones that she was used to causing problems. She explained to them how the Shua Structure System worked, and that they would all be using it in class for the rest of the year, and she told them about the new scented stamp rewards. Julia stumbled slightly while explaining the new program. She remembered that the day before she had pictured herself explaining the new rules and the entire class in revolt with pick axes and torches just like a scene right out of "Frankenstein." Instead, the children listened and afterwards were excited about the stamps. Julia was pleasantly surprised. "So far, so good" she thought.

Later on that day the class started an art project. Chris, one of her "problem students," began to get frustrated because he was having trouble drawing inside the designated lines. His frustration turned to anger and he threw the crayon across the room and yelled out, "I CAN'T DO IT!" and began to cry. The more Julia tried to convince him that he could, the louder he cried. Suddenly Julia noticed that all the children had stopped their projects and focused completely on Chris.

"Here is the chance you were looking for," she told herself. She quit looking at Chris's tear-filled, eyes, focusing on his forehead with her Power Look and said in an authoritative voice, "Chris, that's a *one*."

Chris looked at her in shock. He continued to cry and picked up another crayon, ready to throw. He looked at Julia, her expression was still blank. She was no longer giving him the sympathy he had been looking for, in her tone of voice or her facial expression.

It was difficult for her. She kept reminding herself to focus on his forehead and not his eyes. Then she remembered another technique that she had learned the week before at the preschool. Getting rid of "I can'tism," Angela had called it.

As Chris was about to throw the second crayon, Julia softly spoke up. "Chris, I know that drawing inside the lines can be very hard and can even make you mad," she said.

Chris's angry expression shifted to curious. "I was teaching another boy in a different class the same lesson. He had the same brown hair like yours and he also had a Spiderman shirt just like yours."

Chris looked at his shirt and smiled as Julia continued. "His name was Max and he was getting angry, just like you are right now. Max did not like feeling angry. I told him to use his crayon very slowly when he colored near the edges of the lines, and you know what? He tried it and he was able to keep it in the lines. He did a great job and was so happy afterwards. Do you want to try it?" she asked as she held up her hand for a high-five.

Chris looked at her curiously. Five seconds passed. Those five seconds felt like five hundred to Julia. She began to doubt herself even as she kept her hand up for the high-five. But just as Julia was about to pull her hand away, Chris suddenly smiled, gave her an enthusiastic high-five and nodded his head. He then proceeded to draw very slowly around the edges of the picture. As he did, he was able to keep the color in the lines. The smile on his face extended to his ears as he yelled, "I DID IT!"

"Great job!" Angela said excitedly as Chris traced delicately inside of the lines. She was more excited than Chris. "It worked!" she thought to herself. "It really worked." Julia watched as Chris focused intensely on his project. Once he slipped and his crayon accidently went outside the line. Julia could see the frustration return to his face immediately.

"NO! I can't let him lose his focus," Julia thought. "This 'I can't' has to stop right now."

"Whoever's listening, hands in the air!" she called out quickly. All the children instantaneously raised both hands in the air.

"Chris," she said as he looked at her while the entire class looked at Chris. "When you first started drawing, you said 'I can't do it', right?" Chris nodded.

"Then you got upset and angry. Did you like feeling that way?" Julia asked.

Chris shook his head and said, "No," in a firm voice.

"Then you tried what I told you. Did it work when you tried?"

"Yes!" Chris replied.

"And how did you feel after you were able to keep the colors inside the lines?" Julia continued.

"I felt happy," Chris answered.

"Did you like feeling angry or happy?" Julia asked.

"HAPPY!" Chris exclaimed.

"So next time you say 'I can't,' you're going to say 'I'll try!' instead if you want to feel happy, right?" she asked. Julia needed to make sure that Chris' 'I can't' would not resurface.

"Chris, I want you to think about some other times when you say 'I can't.' Do you sometimes say 'I can't' at home?"

Chris looked up and started to think, then said, "Yes."

"What do you say 'I can't' about at home?" Julia asked.

"When I play soccer with my brothers, I try and kick the ball into the goal and I can't do it." Chris replied.

"And how do you feel?" Julia asked.

"I get really mad and I don't want to play anymore," Chris answered.

"When you said 'I can't' in class before, remember what happened afterward?" Julia asked.

Chris said, "I said, 'I'll try,' and I did it."

"Yes. And remember how you felt after you tried and found out you could do it?" Julia asked.

"I was happy!" Chris said.

"So, if you want to be happy, whenever you say 'I can't' and get mad, say 'I'll try' and be happy."

Chris said "OK."

114

Julia then turned her attention to the entire class. "Everyone, when something is hard to do, do we say 'I can't' and be mad?"

"NO!" they all yelled.

"What do we say?" Julia shouted with excitement.

"I'LL TRY!" the children shouted, laughing.

As Julia looked in their eyes, she could see that some of the children understood, while others were really just repeating her words. She knew that she now had to continuously reinforce the 'I'll try' concept to make it stick. She smiled and imagined the difference it would make in Chris's life if whenever he experienced 'I can'tism' he thought about how unstoppable he would be if he ignored every 'I can't' that crossed his path and said 'I can,' instead.

Life Skills Toolbox

Removing "I can't" from a child's vocabulary can teach that child to attempt anything they want instead of being afraid to try. The "I Can't" doesn't exist in reality but only in the child's mind. Typically at some point the child heard someone tell him that he was unable to do something and he believed it. Teaching children to change "I can't" to "I'll try" is an excellent way to help them recognize the pattern and continuously interrupt and eventually break it.

Replacing "I can't" with "I'll try"

1.   Identify the behavior or action that the child believes he can't do.
2. Tell the child that you UNDERSTAND how hard that action must appear.
3.   MOTIVATE the child by describing another child who resembles him and tell him one new fact that helps him be successful.
4. PRAISE the child for trying even before he has actually tried the new technique, then invite him to try the action.
5. Once the child is successful address him individually or address the entire group of children.
6. Ask the child how he felt when he said "I can't." The child will usually reply with a negative feeling such as "bad" or "sad."
7. Then ask the child how he felt after he tried and

was successful in the action. The child will usually reply with a positive feeling such as "happy" or "good."

8. Ask the child if he wants to feel "sad" or "happy." Most children will reply with "happy."

9. Ask, "Did you feel happy when you said 'I can't" or when you tried?' The usual response is 'When I tried.'"

10. Ask the child, "If we want to feel happy, do we say 'I can't,' or 'I'll try?'" The usual response is "I'll try."

11. Ask the child to think about other times when he has said, "I can't," and coach him so that he will visualize the more positive experience that will occur when he say 'I'll try,' in this circumstance, also.

Chapter 13: Confidence

Over the next five months Julia implemented the Shua Structure System in her classroom. She was tested in the beginning. Danny was sent to the principal's office after receiving a *four* two days in a row. The second time, Julia almost didn't send him down, but Angela's voice popped in her head saying, "Follow through every time."

The next day he came into the classroom a different child. Julia found out the principal had had a meeting with Danny's parents and convinced them to institute consequences at home if Danny was sent to the principal's office again. Danny was upset at Julia. But as soon as he walked into the classroom with an obviously angry expression on his face, Julia told him that if he was a good listener in the beginning of class, she would make him the chalk board writer in math class. Danny's frown turned into a smile. He liked writing on the board. He liked the feeling of importance he got as the one chosen to stand in front of the class and write the answers, and Julia knew that.

Danny was a good listener that day and received his reward. As he wrote everyone's answers on the board Danny knew that a lot of the attention was on him. He smiled and became very excited. In fact, he got so excited that he took a piece of chalk and threw it on the ground. Immediately Julia gave him the Power Look. "That's a *one*," she said.

Danny picked up the chalk and changed his expression immediately.

"Pattern interrupted!" Julia told herself excitedly. Danny had been able to stop himself before his moment of anger turned into a full blown tantrum.

Julia called out another math equation and gave Danny a high-five for writing the answers quickly. He smiled excitedly after the high five and finished the class with only a *one*. That day he got his first smelly stamp reward.

In a few weeks Danny's behavior had changed so markedly that he became one of Julia's permanent helpers. Eventually everyone in the class received some sort of helper title. Danny went to the principal's office only one more time that year. He was invited to Mr. Michaels' office to receive a gold medal that read "Most Improved" along with a gift certificate for his family to the local pizzeria.

Julia even suggested that Danny's parents develop a positive reinforcer at home for his continued good behavior. From that point on Danny worked harder in school and even joined the soccer and chess clubs.

When Danny's parents came in for parent-teacher conferences towards the end of the year his mother jumped towards Julia and hugged her. With tears in her eyes she said, "You have done miracles with Danny. All of your coaching has shown us how to help him at home and keep him focused on positive activities. He never stops talking about you. We can't thank you enough!"

Julia felt the tears swelling in her own eyes as she said, "It's taken all of us," Julia replied.

The school year was almost over and Julia was on her way to the Choice School for Zachary's graduation ceremony. He would move to kindergarten in the fall and she thought about the changes that he had been through during the last year. The same rules and systems used at his school that helped him learn to talk instead of cry had helped Julia's criers stop crying in her class, too. She thought back to Danny who at the beginning of the year would become angry and disruptive almost daily.

Once Danny had consistently begun showing positive behavior, Julia tried the projection technique with him to see if she could learn why he acted out. During her conversation she learned that he was often getting bullied by his older brother. He also told her that he felt that his baby sister got all of his mom's attention. His acting out was really an attempt to get more attention from his mother. When he misbehaved at school, his mother was called in. When she was at the school talking with him and with his teachers, he knew she wasn't focused on the baby.

Julia discovered that Danny loved to express himself through percussion instruments and mom bought him a drum set for the garage as a reward for good behavior. Julia joked with his mother about wanting tickets when his band accepted a Grammy some day. Danny's mother thanked her and said, "You never know."

Mr. Michaels was also very impressed. Julia had not only managed to help out Danny by refocusing his energy, she had also stopped Chris from constantly crying in the face of discomfort and fear. Even though Julia's first instinct was to baby Chris, she stuck to her commitment and Chris slowly stopped crying and began communicating with words, rather than tears.

Mr. Michaels was also very impressed with Julia's ability to invite the children's parents to try the same techniques at home. Julia knew that the at-home reinforcement was a large factor in the overall behavioral changes in the children. Mr. Michaels was happy. Danny's parents were happy.

Chris's parents were happy. Julia was happy. Mr. Michaels shocked Julia during the last week of school when he asked if she would run a teacher workshop for the rest of the school staff.

As she pulled up to the Choice School she saw Angela greeting parents. Of course, Angela was smiling.

"Angela, I just want to thank you again for everything you've done. I know I have said this before, but the information that I've learned from you, your teachers and your school is extraordinary. I have a completely new perspective on how to teach children, and now I understand that forcing a child or an adult to do anything doesn't work. Once they choose to do something on their own, then they can own it. They are responsible for it and they try their best. I learned a very important lesson. If you really want to understand somebody, or you want to take care of an argument or a situation, put yourself in the other person's shoes. If you put yourself in their shoes, an entire new world opens up.

"I've tried to teach choice to my children every day and the results are amazing. So amazing that not only did my principal commend me, he wants me to teach other teachers your philosophy. He wants me to train them and create a program that implements these skills and philosophies inside the school's curriculum," Julia said.

"Imagine an elementary school that works with the Choice School philosophy. Imagine a school without Shyers, Criers, or undisciplined children. Imagine a school where teaching and education was taught and learned without distractions or negativity. That is what I want to see," she added.

Angela smiled and said, "Then do it. Create that school. Create an entire school that works with the teachers and parents keeping the children in mind. It will help so many children and teachers alike."

Julia was taken aback. "I can't do that," she said. But even as the words came out of her mouth, she realized what she had said, and began to laugh.

"A wise lady once said, don't say 'I can't,' say 'I'll try!'" said Angela.

Julia laughed and said, "Okay, I will try."

"I am truly happy for you and your students," added Angela. You should come back here this summer since you have the time off. There is so much more to learn. Now let's go and say hello to your graduating boy. It's his big day."

They walked to get Zachary and Olivia and went outside for the school's graduation ceremony.

"It feels like my graduation, too," she thought to herself. Her eyes connected with Zachary's and Olivia put her head down in her lap. Zachary waved to her as she waved back.

Final Thoughts

Writing this book was an adventure for me and I hope that you enjoyed reading it as much as I enjoyed writing it. Remember to try on the Shua Structure System ideas like a pair of shoes. Try them on and walk around in them for a little while. If you don't like some of them, or you feel they don't work for you, don't use them. However please give them a try. There is only one way that you and your children will not benefit from these ideas, and that is if you keep them to yourself and do not try them at all. Be brave. If you want this to work, it will work. Congratulations on finishing the first step in your journey to learn how to help children succeed powerfully in life. Give yourself a high-five.

About the Authors

During his career, **Ron Shuali**, founder of Shua Life Skills, has effectively helped thousands of children to become physically and mentally fit. A Rutgers University graduate, he has devoted years to studying philosophy, psychology and other modalities in order to understand the mind, with a special focus on children, and their development. He is an entrepreneur and author of numerous articles.

Ron is a black belt martial arts instructor, certified personal trainer, former professional wrestler, FIT™ master instructor, reiki master, and public speaker and member of the National Speakers Association. He has presented his workshops at the NAEYC, NJSACC and at the New Jersey Education Association (NJEA) Conference.

Ron and his team teach numerous preschool through fifth grade fitness programs such as Yogarate, Fitness, Yoga, Karate and Soccer. He heads up children's assembly programs on Breaking the Bully Circle, Outsmarting the Stranger, and Fun Fitness. Teachers can earn professional development hours by attending Ron's workshops, Bringing Respect Back to the Schools, Body & Mind, Effective Transitioning, Bullying 101 and Outsmart the Stranger For Adults.

As an active member of Safe Kids Middlesex County (NJ) of the Level One Trauma Center @ Robert Wood Johnson University Hospital, Ron helps raise awareness about conflict resolution and bullying. His pro-bono work with the "New Weigh" program at Robert Wood Johnson University Hospital has helped many children combat childhood obesity and live healthier, happier, longer lives.

David S. Levine, is currently Director of Marketing for a New York City I.T. consulting firm. Prior to that, he was a principal advisor, consultant and certified business coach in his own firm, representing ActionCOACH until 2007. In addition to his work as a business advisor, David was an award-winning adjunct professor at Rutgers University School of Communications and is also a managing partner of Shua Life Skills.

David holds a BS (Banking/Finance & Marketing) and MBA (Marketing & Finance) from New York University. He has been an officer/board member of various industry, educational, and community service organizations, including Highland Park New Jersey Main Street, BNI, and the Chamber of Commerce. He has also sat on the board of directors of a publicly held corporation and is a speaker and panelist at business and industry events. He has been involved in several new business startups where he worked on business plans and strategic planning, as well as raising capital. David is also a United States Patent Holder.

Breinigsville, PA USA
14 September 2009
223961BV00005B/2/P